PENGUIN PASSNOTES

The Woman in White

Peter Broad was educated at Sidney Sussex College, Cambridge, and took a Post Graduate Certificate of Education at Oxford. Since then he has taught English and Drama at Latymer Upper School, Hammersmith, and spent three years as a professional actor, appearing in London, on tour and at Ludlow Castle. He is currently teaching at Shrewsbury School.

PENGUIN PASSNOTES

WILKIE COLLINS

The Woman in White

PETER BROAD
ADVISORY EDITOR: S. H. COOTE, M.A., PH.D.

PENGUIN BOOKS

Penguin Books Ltd, Harmondsworth, Middlesex, England
Penguin Books, 40 West 23rd Street, New York, New York 10010, U.S.A.
Penguin Books Australia Ltd, Ringwood, Victoria, Australia
Penguin Books Canada Ltd, 2801 John Street, Markham, Ontario, Canada L3R 1B4
Penguin Books (N.Z.) Ltd, 182–190 Wairau Road, Auckland 10, New Zealand

First published 1984

Copyright © Peter Broad, 1984
All rights reserved

Made and printed in Great Britain by
Richard Clay (The Chaucer Press) Ltd, Bungay, Suffolk
Filmset in 10/12 Ehrhardt by
Northumberland Press Ltd, Gateshead

*The publishers are grateful to the following Examination Boards for
permission to reproduce questions from examination papers used in
individual titles in the Passnotes series:*

*Associated Examining Board, University of Cambridge Local Examinations
Syndicate, Joint Matriculation Board, University of London School
Examinations Department, Oxford and Cambridge Schools Examination
Board, University of Oxford Delegacy of Local Examinations.*

*The Examination Boards accept no responsibility whatsoever for the
accuracy or method of working in any suggested answers given as models.*

Contents

To the Student

This book is designed to help you with your O-level or C.S.E. English Literature examinations. It contains a synopsis of the plot, a glossary of the more unfamiliar words and phrases, and a commentary on some of the issues raised by the text. An account of the writer's life is also included as background.

The page references in parentheses refer to the Penguin English Library edition, edited by Julian Symons.

When you use this book remember that it is no more than an aid to your study. It will help you find passages quickly and perhaps give you some ideas for essays. But remember: *This book is not a substitute for reading the text and it is your response and your knowledge that matter.* These are the things the examiners are looking for, and they are also the things that will give you the most pleasure. Show your knowledge and appreciation to the examiner, and show them clearly.

Introduction: The Life and Background of Wilkie Collins

Wilkie Collins was born in London in 1824, the eldest son of William Collins, R.A. (Royal Academician – a society of artists now based in Piccadilly). His unusual Christian name was taken from his father's friend, sponsor and fellow-painter, Sir David Wilkie; Collins always used it himself and was addressed by it. He went to a private school in Highbury where he was by all accounts a poor scholar, often singled out for punishment by the masters, and then spent two years in Italy with his parents. His experiences in Italy he put to good use in his first novel, *Antonina* (finally published 1850), a historical piece set in ancient Rome. Wilkie Collins then became an apprentice in the London firm of Antrobus & Co., which dealt in the tea trade; subsequently, his father arranged for him to leave business and enter Lincoln's Inn to study law. Before he was called to the Bar in 1851, William Collins died, and Collins's first published work was a two-volume biography of his father, which appeared in 1848. Wilkie Collins was a gifted artist, having exhibited a landscape painting at the Royal Academy, and, at one time, contemplated following his father (compare Walter Hartright's father). However, after the relative success of *Rambles Beyond Railways* and following his friendship with Charles Dickens in the 1850s, he was dedicated to a literary career.

Meeting Dickens was easily the most significant event in Collins's life: they became very good friends, they went abroad together (almost certainly visiting brothels as well as the more cultural haunts), they corresponded (although only Dickens's letters survive; Collins's were destroyed by Dickens as an act of principle to prevent the 'improper use of confidential letters'), and they collaborated on several writing projects. Dickens was to appear, highly successfully, in his friend's play *The Frozen Deep* (1857); Collins was to become a most valuable contributor to his friend's magazines *All the Year Round* and *Household Words*. In some ways, it appears an unequal friendship, with Dickens the self-evident genius, Collins the journeyman hack; but it is clear they valued each other in personal terms. Collins's ability to construct a complex but satisfying plot was a skill which Dickens admired and may even have been trying to emulate in his last, unfinished, novel, *Edwin Drood*. In Dickens, Collins found an editor willing to publish *The Woman in White* in the magazine in which Dickens had serialized his own novel, *A Tale of Two Cities*. The confidence shown by his editor was amply rewarded: sales of the magazine increased and a popular success was assured. As the Penguin introduction states:

Queues formed outside the offices to buy the next instalment, cloaks, bonnets, perfumes, waltzes and quadrilles were called by the book's title. Gladstone cancelled a theatre engagement to go on reading it, and Prince Albert sent a copy to Baron Stockmar. When it was published between covers, in the three-volume form of the day, four editions were published in a month. Throughout Europe and in the United States, the novel had a comparable success. Before it, Wilkie Collins had been one among a hundred Victorian writers making a reasonable living. After *The Woman in White*, he was a famous and sought-after novelist. (pp. 15–16)

His subsequent novels – *No Name* (1862), *Armadale* (1866) and *The Moonstone* (1868) – were equally successful with the public and financially satisfying to Collins: in one year, he earned more than £10,000. His ability to write to order for serial publication and his skill in turning out lively occasional articles were now enhanced by his reputation as the master of a new genre, the 'sensation novel'. The public was clearly impressed but, in general, the press and the critics were not. He rarely received good reviews, and many were outright hostile to his work. He took comfort in his popularity, but did not miss an opportunity to reply to his critics in his Preface to the second edition of *The Woman in White*. The slightly defensive tone of the writing cannot conceal his pride in his book's success or his sense of frustration at his critical unpopularity. In fact, Collins has had to wait until the twentieth century for a heavyweight critic to champion his work. T. S. Eliot, in his essay 'Wilkie Collins and Dickens', commends *The Woman in White*, especially for the characters of Marian and Count

Fosco, but goes on to recommend *The Moonstone* for being 'the best balanced between plot and character' and *Armadale* as the novel 'which reaches the greatest melodramatic intensity' (T. S. Eliot, *Selected Essays*, Faber, 1932).

In 1873–4, Collins visited America to give a series of public readings of his work, just as Dickens had done. Usually he chose to read his short story 'The Frozen Deep'. It was in America, some ten years later, that his play *Rank and Riches* enjoyed a successful run, having failed when it was produced at the Adelphi in London. Both he and Dickens sought after theatrical success; Collins adapted *Armadale* twice, *No Name*, *The Woman in White* and *The New Magdalen* for the stage with varying degrees of success, while Dickens had to wait for the Royal Shakespeare Company in the 1980s before enjoying a stage hit on both sides of the Atlantic.

His later novels make strange reading nowadays. *Poor Miss Finch* is based on the love of two identical twins for the same blind girl, while his creation of Miserimus Dexter, the crippled poet of *The Law and the Lady*, breaks new melodramatic ground even for Collins. At the same time, his health, never robust, began to fail him. In the course of writing *The Moonstone*, he wrote,

My suffering was so great ... that I could not control myself and keep quiet. My cries and groans so deeply distressed my amanuensis [secretary] to whom I was dictating, that he could not continue his work and had to leave me. After that I employed several other men, with the same result: no one of them could stand the strain.

Eventually, a young woman proved able to cope with his fits and the occasions he 'lay on the couch writhing and groaning'. The cause of his agony was probably a form of rheumatism and his only relief from it came in the form of laudanum (a pain-killing draught in which opium was the chief ingredient), which he took in ever-increasing quantities until his death. He was almost certainly an addict in his later years, a factor which may not have improved his writing. Towards the end of his life, he became something of a recluse. He was upset by the death of his friend, and angry at John Forster's *Life of Charles Dickens* – which he re-titled 'The Life of John Forster, with Occasional

Anecdotes by Charles Dickens'. He died at 82 Wimpole Street on 23 September 1889, and was buried five days later in Kensal Green Cemetery.

His private life was a subject which provoked interest and comment until his death. He lived at home with his mother until he was thirty-two years old, and was a member of a circle of friends that included the artists Millais and Holman Hunt. When he left home, it was not to marry but to set up with a girl in her twenties, Caroline Graves, who had a daughter and a husband whose whereabouts were unknown. His decision was not approved by all his friends: on his tour to Italy with Dickens, the latter had remarked, 'He occasionally expounds a code of morals taken from French novels which I instantly and with becoming gravity smash' (quoted by Angus Wilson in *The World of Charles Dickens*, Penguin Books, 1970). Socially, he was less respectable and less welcome than before: as a result, his name does not feature frequently in the circumspect memoirs of his contemporaries. In fact, he never married Caroline, or Martha Rudd, his other mistress, who bore him three children. The explanation for his unorthodox life-style is hard to explain, just as it is hard to explain the fact that he arranged Caroline's marriage to another man, a plumber named Clow, and, when that marriage failed, returned to live with her again. According to a friend, 'His eye seems to have roved in search of romance whenever he crossed the threshold of his home to set foot in London streets.' In his will, however, he left half the income from his estate to Caroline and her daughter Lizzie, and half to Martha Rudd and their three children: it gives us no further clue to his relationship with them or, indeed, anyone else.

What of Collins's literary legacy? *The Moonstone* has been called the first great English detective story and *The Woman in White* has survived to be read by thousands and enjoyed by millions in the excellent BBC television adaptation (if it is repeated, note how its original serial form suits the new medium). If the accolades showered on his friend Dickens have eluded him, at least two of his novels are read, enjoyed and admired nearly a century after his death.

Synopsis of The Woman in White

First Epoch

The story begun by Walter Hartright

Walter Hartright, a London drawing master, visits his widowed mother and sister in Hampstead and there meets his old Italian friend, Professor Pesca. Pesca, whom Walter once saved from drowning, has heard that a Cumberland gentleman, Frederick Fairlie, needs a drawing master for four months. Slightly reluctantly, Walter applies and is accepted for this lucrative post. Walking home across Hampstead, Walter encounters 'the woman in white' – Anne Catherick (pp. 47–54). She is distressed and has a grievance against an unnamed baronet (Sir Percival); she speaks also of having been happy at Limmeridge, Walter's destination in Cumberland. Walter helps her to find a carriage but does not help the two men pursuing her, who inform him she has escaped from an asylum.

After a delayed journey to Limmeridge, only the servants are there to greet Walter; he goes to bed and wakes to enjoy the fine view. Next morning he meets Marian Halcombe (pp. 58–62), whose intelligence and vivacity compensate for her facial ugliness. She is to be one of his two pupils, and the other is Laura Fairlie, her half-sister – their late mother having married twice. Walter tells Marian of his strange encounter and her curiosity is aroused; she decides to examine her mother's correspondence for any clues. Walter is introduced to his eccentric, semi-invalid employer, Mr Frederick Fairlie, who owns a priceless collection of art and lives in fear of any human contact (pp. 65–71). Finally, Walter meets Laura in the summerhouse (pp. 74–5) and is immediately struck by her beauty; by the close of their first day together, he has fallen in love. Marian has found a reference to Anne Catherick in one of her mother's letters; she had been a pupil of Mrs Fairlie for a time, and had proclaimed that she 'will always wear white as long as I live' in gratitude to her teacher. While reading the description of Mrs Fairlie's strange pupil, Marian and Walter observe a resemblance between Laura Fairlie and Anne Catherick.

Walter's feeling for Laura is returned, but suddenly (p. 90) Laura begins to behave more formally and coolly; the once happy trio begin to behave awkwardly together and, finally, Marian explains the reason to Walter. Laura is engaged – an arrangement sanctioned by her father, whose memory Laura reveres, on his deathbed. Walter cannot bear to stay any longer and a diplomatic departure for him is arranged by the resourceful Marian. Laura's fiancé is a baronet from Hampshire, Sir Percival Glyde, and this provides a curious link with Anne Catherick's words. Meanwhile, Laura has received an anonymous letter describing a dream, warning her not to marry Sir Percival; internal evidence suggests to Marian and Walter that the author of the letter is Anne Catherick. The letter had been delivered by an elderly woman.

Walter and Marian decide to make inquiries in the village. They learn, from a schoolboy in disgrace, that the ghost of 'Mistress Fairlie', dressed all in white, has been seen in the churchyard. Walter discovers that Mrs Fairlie's grave has been partially cleaned and decides to watch that night; perhaps the job will be completed. Hiding in the church porch, Walter sees Anne arrive with another woman and start to clean. Carefully, he introduces himself to her again, reminding her of their previous encounter (pp. 118–19). He discovers Anne dislikes her own mother and wrote the letter to Laura; but, at the mention of Sir Percival, she begins to scream and he learns no more, although he is now certain Sir Percival (the baronet) put her away in the asylum.

Walter tells Marian his discoveries and they visit Todd's Corner farm, where Anne has been staying, but she has left that morning with her companion, Mrs Clements. Marian assures Walter that Sir Percival will have to satisfy both Mr Gilmore, their solicitor, and herself of his good character before marrying Laura. Mr Gilmore arrives, confident the letter is only a slight hiccup in the proceedings – he has sent a copy to Sir Percival's solicitor and set about tracing Anne and Mrs Clements. Walter's last evening at Limmeridge is a tense re-creation of earlier and happier occasions (pp. 143–7) and, next morning, he leaves, pledging friendship to Marian and promising to write; Laura's parting gift to him is a sketch of the summerhouse where they first met.

The story continued by Vincent Gilmore

Sir Percival arrives and Mr Gilmore is favourably impressed by his straightforward manner and his explanation that Anne Catherick was placed in an asylum with her own mother's approval and at his own expense; the grudge borne against him is explicable. Sir Percival challenges Marian to write to Mrs Catherick; and the reply swiftly and tersely confirms his story. Nevertheless, Marian's doubts persist and she confides them to Mr Gilmore; he takes them seriously out of regard for her. Laura wants to delay the marriage, and keeps to her room to avoid Sir Percival. Mr Gilmore visits her there and tries to explain the settlement. Laura is deaf to his efforts, but insists Marian live with her after the marriage and reveals her desire to make a personal bequest in her will (to Walter, p. 166). Mr Gilmore leaves, uneasy in his own mind.

Eight days later, Mr Gilmore is informed the marriage will take place before the end of the year. He explains the settlement in detail to Laura. Two key sums of money are involved: (1) £10,000, which Mme Fosco, Laura's aunt, would receive if Laura died before her; (2) £20,000, which Sir Percival, her husband, would receive if Laura died before him childless. Mr Gilmore is very unhappy about the second item: he has discovered that Sir Percival has large debts and virtually no income. He finds himself under pressure to settle from Mr Merriman, Sir Percival's solicitor, and gains no support from Laura's guardian, Mr Fairlie. On his way to make a last-minute, personal appeal to Mr Fairlie, he meets Walter by chance near Holborn. Walter is distressed by the loss of his beloved and her imminent wedding, and fears he may be the victim of Sir Percival's sleuths. He is about to start a new life abroad (pp. 178–9) as an artist attached to an archaeological excavation in Central America. Mr Gilmore's appeal predictably fails and he is left regretting he can do no more to help Laura.

The story continued by Marian Halcombe

Laura summons the courage to tell Sir Percival she can never love him, although she would always be a dutiful wife. Sir Percival will not release her, claiming her honesty has made her yet more attractive, and leaves to prepare his Hampshire home for her arrival. Marian and Laura spend a few days on holiday at the home of Yorkshire friends, before being summoned back – the wedding has been fixed for 22 December.

Marian keeps Walter's journey to Honduras a secret from Laura; Laura begs Marian to keep the wedding a secret from him. Blackwater Park, Sir Percival's home, is being renovated, and so the couple are to spend the winter in Italy after the wedding. Count Fosco, Sir Percival's friend, and Mme Fosco, Laura's aunt, will join them there. Sir Percival consents to Marian's living with them at Blackwater. The wedding day is 'a wild, unsettled morning', and Marian is left distraught.

The Second Epoch

The story continued by Marian Halcombe

Marian is at Blackwater Park, awaiting the return of the Glydes from Italy, and also the Foscos, who are to be guests for the summer. Laura's letters have avoided all mention of her marriage: Marian has forebodings. Her curiosity to meet the Count is excited by Laura's description of the improvement wrought in their aunt, Mme Fosco, by her husband. Exploring the grounds of the ugly house (much inferior to Limmeridge), Marian finds a dying spaniel, apparently owned by Mrs Catherick, which has been shot by the gamekeeper. Despite Marian's and the housekeeper's attention, it dies – a worrying omen.

The Glydes and Foscos arrive and are described by Marian (pp. 233–47): Laura is under stress, Sir Percival is yet more irritable,

Mme Fosco is oddly subservient and Count Fosco is bizarre and fascinating. Mr Merriman, Sir Percival's solicitor, arrives unexpectedly. Marian discovers Sir Percival's dire financial crisis and reveals it to Laura. Sir Percival orders everybody to the library, only to take a walk to the lake instead. There, Fosco discourses, elegantly and chillingly, on 'successful' crime, and notices the spaniel's blood. Marian reveals that Mrs Catherick has visited the house; this arouses Sir Percival's unconcealed anger, which even Fosco is unable to subdue. The meeting in the library is reconvened, and Laura is asked to sign a document, with the Foscos and Marian as witnesses; Sir Percival refuses to reveal the contents of the document: Laura refuses to sign until he does so, as does Marian. Marian writes to Mr Kyrle (Mr Gilmore's partner) and puts the letter in the postbag, only to be escorted away for an unprecedented walk with Mme Fosco. On her return, Marian sees the Count putting a letter in the bag and, re-examining her envelope, finds it is not properly stuck down.

Walking in the grounds after dinner, Laura reveals to Marian the true misery of her marriage. Moreover, Sir Percival has discovered, by accident, that it is Walter whom Laura loves, and he has vowed 'You shall repent it' (p. 283). They spot a slowly moving figure in the white mist, perhaps female, certainly frightening (p. 285). Back inside, Marian establishes it could not have been the Count, his wife or the servants. Laura has lost a brooch and, searching the grounds, meets Anne Catherick – the figure they had seen in the mist, and, fearing they are being watched, arranges a second meeting next day. At the park gates, Marian receives a reply from Mr Kyrle; he suggests he sees the document before it is signed. Fosco surprises her and Marian is now certain he and Sir Percival are allies. Laura goes to keep her appointment with Anne; Marian follows later to allay suspicion. She cannot find Laura and, back at the house, hears she has been imprisoned in her own room by a furious Sir Percival. Eventually gaining admission to the room, in part thanks to the unlikely and suspicious support of Mme Fosco, she learns Laura's second meeting with Anne had never taken place. The Count had spied on their first, and Anne had left a warning note for Laura buried in the sand (p. 320), which Sir Percival had intercepted. The note mentioned a 'secret', and he had imprisoned Laura in a great rage, convinced she knew more than she was telling. Marian writes to Mr Kyrle again, using Fanny, Laura's dismissed maid, as a messenger – the postbag is no longer safe.

Marian takes the letters, one addressed to Mr Kyrle, the other to Mr Fairlie, to Fanny at the inn and fears she may have been followed. Writing her journal, Marian overhears the Count and Sir Percival in the garden. Bravely she perches above the open windows of the library to eavesdrop on their conversation. She learns the extent of Sir Percival's and the Count's financial crises, that her letters have been intercepted and that the Count clearly dominates the partnership: they would receive £30,000 between them were Laura to die childless. Despite pressure put on him, Sir Percival will not reveal his 'secret', admitting only that Anne Catherick is crucial to it and that she must be found. Fosco pledges his help and, on hearing of Anne's remarkable resemblance to Laura, leaves in a state of near-elation. Marian has been soaked by the rain while she has been listening, and just manages to record all the details before fever grips her (Count Fosco adds a postscript full of admiration for Marian and confidence in his plans, pp. 358–60).

The story continued by Frederick Fairlie
Under duress, Mr Fairlie describes Fanny's visit and retells her story: how she had been visited at the inn by Mme Fosco, had taken tea with her, fainted and woken up alone to find her letters crumpled. Marian's letter to Mr Fairlie had suggested Laura take refuge from her wayward husband at Limmeridge. Mr Fairlie's response is that Marian should come on her own at first to discuss the proposed visit. Mr Fairlie has also received a letter from a worried Mr Kyrle: inside an envelope with Marian's handwriting on it, he has found a blank sheet of paper. Fosco arrives and the two most outrageous eccentrics meet face to face (pp. 369–78). With a typical mixture of charm, intelligence and will-power, Fosco manipulates Mr Fairlie, who accepts his plan: Laura is to be invited immediately, even as Marian recovers, and her journey is to be broken in London at the Foscos' home in St John's Wood; Fosco himself will put her on the train to

Cumberland next day. The briefest of invitations is penned by Mr Fairlie, certain his niece would never leave Blackwater without Marian.

The story continued by Eliza Michelson, housekeeper at Blackwater Park
Mrs Michelson, the God-fearing housekeeper, describes Marian's fever and Fosco's efforts to treat it. These efforts meet with the contempt of Mr Dawson, the local doctor; he is suspicious of all foreigners. Much to Mr Dawson's disapproval, Fosco arranges a nurse for Marian, a Mrs Rubelle, who is also foreign. So far as Mrs Michelson can see (as it proves, not very far), she is honest. While Fosco is in London, Marian has a relapse. On his return, the Count fears it may be typhus. Mr Dawson disagrees, but a London doctor confirms Fosco's diagnosis. Ten anxious days later, Marian improves; Laura meanwhile declines. After another argument with Fosco, Mr Dawson is dismissed, as are all the staff except Mrs Michelson herself and the horrendous Margaret Porcher. Mrs Michelson is sent to Torquay, ostensibly to find convalescent rooms for Marian and Laura. In fact, Blackwater Park is now safe for Fosco to execute his plans for Laura's 'death'. On her return, Mrs Michelson is told that the Foscos have left for London, apparently taking Marian with them. Laura, distressed to be parted from Marian, decides to follow and Sir Percival arranges for Fosco to meet her at the station in London. On her return, Mrs Michelson discovers Marian has been concealed at Blackwater all the time; she has been tricked and Laura is alone and in Fosco's hands. Although she immediately resigns, Mrs Michelson stays on to look after Marian. During that night, Sir Percival grows wild, gallops away and takes the morning train to an unknown destination. Mrs Michelson and Marian leave Blackwater together, the latter on her way to Limmeridge. Unfortunately, she cannot remember the date of Laura's departure.

The story continued in several narratives
Hester Pinhorn, Fosco's illiterate cook, relates the arrival of the sick 'Lady Glyde' (Anne Catherick), the doctor's diagnosis of heart disease, her apparent recovery next day and her sudden relapse and death that evening. She can find no fault in her master or his actions. The doctor's

certificate of death is reproduced, including the date – 25 July 1850 – which is a vital clue for Walter in his subsequent investigations. Jane Gould, who prepared the body for the coffin and saw the lid screwed down, swears to those facts. Then follows the tombstone inscription – this is, of course, altered eventually to record Anne's death and fulfil her wish to be buried alongside Mrs Fairlie (p. 639).

The narrative of Walter Hartright

Walter has returned to London, having escaped death several times, as foretold in Marian's dream (pp. 295–7), and learns from his mother of Laura's 'death'. He travels to her grave at Limmeridge and sees two women approaching it; one is recognizably Marian, the other, incredibly, Laura (p. 431).

The Third Epoch

The story continued by Walter Hartright

A week later. Walter is living with his two 'sisters' in poverty in an obscure part of London. He is determined to establish Laura's identity, but first he tells Marian's story. Marian learnt of Laura's 'death' at Blackwater Park, but was unable to consult Mr Kyrle in London until three weeks had passed. He was of little help as the facts seemed to be plain. At Limmeridge, Mr Fairlie had been warned by Fosco that Anne, safe in the asylum, is under the illusion she is Lady Glyde. This clue had sent Marian straight to the asylum, where, recognizing Laura, she bribed the nurse and secured her release. Laura remembered little of her ordeal, except for a vague recollection of being attended by Mrs Rubelle. They returned to Limmeridge together. Predictably, Mr Fairlie had not recognized his niece and, with the asylum authorities in pursuit, they had decided to go on to London. They had stopped at the graveyard on the way and met Walter there by chance, so changing the course of all their lives (p. 451).

Walter takes a poorly paid job and, pooling his savings with Marian, they determine to prove Laura's identity and expose the crime of which she is the victim. Slowly they nurse her back to health; since her time in the asylum, her resemblance to Anne has become all the more marked. Walter visits Mr Kyrle and finds the law will be of little help to him; he must pursue matters himself. Walter, who has been followed home, brings Marian a letter from Fosco, which warns them both not to pursue their inquiries. He ignores the threat and visits Blackwater Park in an attempt to establish the date of Laura's journey to London and the contents of Sir Percival's 'secret'. He is unsuccessful on both counts and meets a suspicious man in the grounds, who tries to provoke an argument. Home again, Marian suggests Mrs Clements may prove informative, and Walter seeks her out.

Mrs Clements describes Anne's determination to meet Laura, even though she was ill. She tells Walter how, after one of their meetings, Anne had become very ill and she (Mrs Clements) had gone in her place to the boathouse and met Fosco. Fosco's message, supposedly from Laura, told them to return to London where Laura would make contact. Fosco had given Anne some medical treatment, and she had made a spectacular recovery. In London, they received no communication from Laura until an elderly lady (Mme Fosco) delivered a message. Mrs Clements had left with her in a cab, only to be abandoned, and to discover on her return that Anne was missing, kidnapped (p. 484).

Next, Mrs Clements reveals Mrs Catherick's history: her marriage to a man she had long spurned; her alleged affair with Sir Percival and her attempt to regain respectability. Having told Mrs Clements of Anne's death, Walter obtains Mrs Catherick's address and leaves to visit her next.

Mrs Catherick is shaken (pp. 504–11) by mention of her husband and by Walter's refusal to believe the common rumour that Sir Percival is Anne's father, but she reveals nothing. Walter is still being followed when he goes to the vestry at Old Welmingham Church. He examines the church register, and sees the entry recording Sir Felix Glyde's marriage squeezed on to the bottom of a page. He decides to look at the duplicate register in Knowlesbury, five miles away, in order to compare the two. On his way, Walter is trapped into assaulting one of his pursuers, and is remanded in custody for three days (this is Sir Percival's ploy to gain time). Walter is freed that afternoon – Mr Dawson, the doctor, has stood bail. When he inspects the duplicate register, Walter finds no matching entry: Sir Percival's parents were not married; he is illegitimate, has a false claim to his title and has forged the record at Old Welmingham. Returning to the Old Welmingham vestry, Walter finds it on fire. Sir Percival dies inside, burnt with the evidence of his secret, despite Walter's attempts to save him (pp. 535–41, a vivid and dramatic scene).

During the inquest Walter keeps Sir Percival's secret. He then receives a letter from Mrs Catherick. In it, she explains how Sir Percival had courted her with gifts in order to obtain the keys to the vestry, and how she had learnt his 'secret' and watched him forge the entry in the register (p. 552). He had refused to clear her name, but paid her 'a handsome yearly allowance', insisting she remain at Welmingham. She reveals how Anne accidentally learnt of 'the secret', without really knowing its contents, and frightened Sir Percival with it – hence his insistence she be put away. Mrs Catherick, never fond of her daughter, did not object.

Marian writes to tell Walter she and Laura have moved to Fulham. Suspecting Fosco's influence, he takes the train to London. Marian has indeed been threatened by Fosco and has seen the asylum owner in the street below, hence their hasty move. Marian tells Laura of Sir Percival's death and Walter reaches the conclusion that Anne's father was Philip Fairlie, which explains their strong resemblance to each other. With Marian's blessing, Walter and Laura are finally married (p. 582). Sir Percival's estate is left to its original and rightful heir.

Walter is certain Fosco is some sort of spy and follows him to the opera, accompanied by Pesca. Pesca does not recognize Fosco, but Fosco seems to know him; the Count is also recognized by a sinister man with a scar on his left cheek. Pesca reveals his membership of the Brotherhood, a secret political society. Fosco is also a member, it seems, with an identifying mark on the arm (pp. 588–98). Walter writes to Pesca, revealing Fosco as a man false to the Brotherhood, and puts the letter in a sealed envelope with instructions that it is not to be opened before 9 a.m. next day. Having taken this wise precaution, he visits Fosco, noticing the same sinister, scarred man lurking outside. In this great climactic scene (pp. 605–18), Walter confronts

Fosco and obtains a written confession of the Count's plan to substitute Anne for Laura. At first, Fosco considers killing Walter; but he is deterred by the existence of Walter's letter. Not admitting his defeat, he negotiates half an hour to make his escape with his wife, and claims the right to challenge Walter to a duel at a later date. He writes his confession, burns the retrieved letter, and leaves in a cab with his wife. The Count's flamboyant confession forms part of the narrative. It confirms Walter's theories, reveals his passion and admiration for Marian and ends with an assertion of his innocence!

Walter confirms that Laura in fact travelled by brougham to meet Fosco on 26 July, the day after her alleged death. He, Laura, Marian and the coach-driver all travel to Limmeridge to confirm the facts. Mr Fairlie is finally convinced and the inscription on the tombstone is altered to record Anne's death instead. They return to London. On business in Paris, Walter and Pesca pass the morgue and see Fosco lying inside – the scarred man has finally killed him, on behalf of the Brotherhood. Mme Fosco survives to tend his grave and write his biography.

Walter's son is born, Mr Fairlie dies and the Hartright family inherits Limmeridge. Marian will continue to be part of that family.

An Account of the Plot

The First Epoch

Preamble, p. 33
This describes how the story will be told, not by a single narrator, but by a series of key witnesses – 'As the Judge might once have heard it, so the Reader shall hear it now.'

The story begun by Walter Hartright (of Clement's Inn, Teacher of Drawing)

CHAPTER I, *pp. 34–7*

The scene is London in late summer: Walter Hartright is leaving his chambers in Clement's Inn, where he has inherited his father's drawing practice, to visit his widowed mother and only surviving sister, Sarah, in Hampstead, as he does twice a week. His father's prudence in paying large sums into life insurance has left the family secure and independent; Walter however is short of money and slightly depressed.

Their door is opened by Walter's Italian friend, Professor Pesca, whom he had met at 'certain great houses' where Walter taught drawing and Pesca Italian. An eccentric, a political refugee, a near-dwarf with a shadowy past, Pesca loves England and the English, and especially Walter, not least because Walter once saved him from drowning in the sea at Brighton in the course of one of his fervent attempts to copy the English in every way. Consequently Pesca has an overwhelming sense of gratitude towards Walter, which he repays quickly and in full, with dramatic repercussions.

CHAPTER II, *pp. 37–46*

Pesca, a favourite of Walter's mother's if not his sister's, obviously has exciting news. Pesca's oratory delays the arrival of the news considerably, but eventually he reveals that one of his employers has a friend, 'Frederick Fairlie Esquire, of Limmeridge House, Cumberland', who needs a drawing master for four months. His tasks are to include the instruction of two young ladies in watercolour painting, and the repair and mounting of a valuable collection of neglected drawings, for four guineas a week. The drawing master would be resident at Limmeridge and 'was to be treated there on the footing of a gentleman'.

Although he is aware of the advantages, Walter is reluctant to apply, but at last submits to pressure from all three and sends his testimonials. Four days later he is accepted by Mr Fairlie, and is to start immediately.

CHAPTER III, *pp. 46–55*

After midnight, having said good-bye to his mother and sister, Walter takes the long way home across Hampstead Heath – London is stiflingly hot. At the crossroads he feels a touch on his shoulder from behind and turns to see a woman in white, who asks him, 'Is that the road to London?' Walter is fairly certain she is genuine, neither a prostitute nor a criminal, and agrees to accompany her to London and not to interfere.

She has a grievance against a baronet, whose name she will not divulge, though she does speak of being 'once happy in Cumberland' – astonishingly, at Limmeridge village, Walter's destination. Her preoccupation with finding a carriage prevents further discussion. Walter finds one and, imploring him not to ask any further questions, she kisses his hand and leaves, her destination unknown.

Walking slowly home, Walter sees a policeman stopped by two men in an open chaise, and hears them ask him if he has seen a woman in white who, they say, has escaped from an asylum.

CHAPTER IV, *pp. 55–7*

Walter is not convinced that the woman in white is insane, though she is clearly strange in her behaviour, and he reaches his lodgings unable to sleep, sketch or read, perplexed by his experiences and his actions.

He takes the train to Carlisle, pleased to be leaving London behind. Engine failure delays his arrival at Limmeridge's nearest station until after 10 p.m., and the family have retired. He eats a solitary supper, having met only the rather disagreeable household servants.

CHAPTER V, *pp. 57–64*

Walter wakes up to a fine view of the distant coast of Scotland and puts the past behind him. He goes down for breakfast and sees, at the window, one of his future pupils, Marian Halcombe. He is impressed by her form and figure, only to be shocked and dismayed by her dark, swarthy, masculine face. Fortunately, her voice, intelligence and wit compensate for her lack of facial beauty and Walter is soon charmed by her humour, self-deprecation and epigrammatic judgements on members of the household, as well as enlightened by her advice. Marian's mother, the late Mrs Fairlie, had married twice and Laura Fairlie – his other pupil – is her half-sister.

Her banter encourages Walter to relate his encounter with the woman in white, and how she spoke fondly of Mrs Fairlie. Marian is intrigued and when Walter is summoned to meet Mr Fairlie, she decides to examine her mother's correspondence for any clues to the identity of the woman in white.

CHAPTER VI, *pp. 64–71*

Walter is shown to his delightful sitting room/studio where he'll work – it has the same view as his bedroom. Next, Mr Fairlie is revealed. He lives in a type of cocoon, first behind a door covered with dark baize and then behind curtains of pale sea-green silk; there is a thick carpet beneath his large easy chair, and he is surrounded by a priceless collection of paintings, china, coins, etchings, furniture, jewellery and watercolours. Walter examines the latter and confirms their value and the need to strain and remount them carefully.

Walter is not charmed by Mr Fairlie. Neither his eccentricity, nor his wealth, nor the 'wretched state of his nerves' (a condition Walter sees as 'selfish affectation'), appeal to him, and he decides not to visit him again unless invited – a mutually agreeable conclusion, it must be added. Before lunch, Walter works on the watercolours, and then goes down in eager anticipation of his first meeting with Laura, and the result of Marian's research.

CHAPTER VII, *pp. 71–87*

At lunch Walter meets Mrs Vesey, Laura's elderly former governess – a monosyllabic, 'vegetable' presence on whom Marian sharpens her wit. To Walter's disappointment Marian has, as yet, found nothing in the letters and he is further disappointed by Laura's absence. She is in a summerhouse in the garden, sketching, when Walter first sees her. For him it is love at first sight and he describes her in detail, using the watercolour drawing he makes later on – though to him it is an inadequate representation of her beauty and blameless character. He senses, also, something incomplete in her which he cannot identify, and he is deeply touched by her remark '... I shall believe all that you say'.

Walter, his two pupils and Mrs Vesey take a drive in an open carriage and, transported by his feelings, he realizes he is in danger of forgetting his position. After dinner, Laura plays Mozart (see p. 81) while Mrs Vesey sleeps and Marian reads. Laura, who is dressed in white, goes on to the terrace to watch the moonlight and on Walter's advice ties a white handkerchief on her head against the night air. Marian calls Walter and reads to him a letter from the late Mrs Fairlie which seems to identify the woman in white as Anne Catherick: while a temporary pupil, she had proclaimed to Mrs Fairlie in gratitude 'I will always wear white as long as I live.'

Walter and the reader are simultaneously made aware of the resemblance between Laura and Anne Catherick – a fact Walter and Marian decide to keep secret from Laura.

CHAPTER VIII, *pp. 87–92*

Laura remembers little of Anne Catherick when questioned by Marian, and cannot confirm Anne's preference for white. Walter admits openly 'I loved her' (Laura). He has been unable to keep his professional distance as he had previously, and now feels keenly the frustration of close contact without the chance to express his emotions. Laura's behaviour suddenly alters. She has become aware of their growing mutual love, and she is now more formal and less relaxed in his company. Awkwardness affects all three and it is finally Marian who breaks the tension.

CHAPTER IX, *pp. 92–100*

Autumn, and as Mrs Vesey perceptively notes 'the winter is coming'! Breakfast is an embarrassingly silent meeting now, in contrast to earlier, happier days; the purple room is to be prepared for a guest on Monday. Marian takes Walter to the garden. On the way she intercepts a letter in strange handwriting for Laura, and eventually lets the gardener's boy take it in. In the summerhouse, the scene of Walter's first meeting with Laura, Marian tells him she is aware of his love for Laura, and although it is mutual, he must try to forget it – not on the grounds of social inequality, but because she is engaged, an arrangement sanctioned by her father on his deathbed. Marian deals kindly with Walter's distress and suggests a good plan for his quick departure from Limmeridge.

Laura's maid tells Marian of Laura's distress, apparently caused by the letter. Walter is anxious to learn the name of Laura's fiancé. It is Sir Percival Glyde, a baronet from Hampshire – a double link with Anne Catherick.

CHAPTER X, *pp. 100–107*

Walter returns to the studio to complete his work for Mr Fairlie, troubled by the connections between Anne Catherick's story of a baronet from Hampshire and Laura's fiancé Sir Percival Glyde, whose home is in Hampshire. Everything seems to lead back to his encounter with the woman in white. He is interrupted by an agitated Marian: the letter to Laura which the gardener's boy had brought in is anonymous and libels Sir Percival. It describes a dream of Laura's wedding, in which the husband (identifiable as Sir Percival by his age, his cough and a scar) has a heart 'as black as night' and warns Laura of the danger in such a match. Laura is distressed and Marian asks Walter, as a friend, to help. They agree it is written by a woman who is probably deranged and its final words – 'Your mother's daughter has a tender place in my heart – for your mother was my first, my best, my only friend' – seem incredibly to point to Anne Catherick. Marian defends Sir Percival's honour, but agrees to join Walter in making inquiries in the village to discover the identity of the elderly woman who delivered the letter.

CHAPTER XI, *pp. 107–16*

Three villagers have seen the woman, but they cannot agree on a
description or the direction she was walking. Marian and Walter decide
to ask the schoolmaster, Mr Dempster, whom they find putting a boy
in disgrace for resolutely asserting that he has seen a ghost. Almost by
chance they question the boy, Jacob Postlethwaite, and he maintains
the ghost which he's seen in the churchyard is that of 'Mistress Fairlie'
dressed all in white. Walter is convinced the letter-writer, the ghost
and the woman in white are the same person, Anne Catherick; and
he confides his theory to Marian.

Walter visits the churchyard, while Marian goes home to Laura.
Mrs Fairlie's grave has been partially cleaned and not, as he establishes,
by the sexton or his wife. Walter decides to watch over the grave that
night to see if the cleaning is continued. At Limmeridge he watches
Laura from his window, unnoticed, as she walks forlornly among the
fallen leaves. At sunset he leaves to begin his vigil over the grave.

CHAPTER XII, *pp. 116–30*

After hiding for half an hour in the church porch Walter hears footsteps
and a female voice confirming to her companion that 'the letter' has
been safely delivered. The younger woman, whose white gown is
visible beneath her cloak, is left to clean the grave. Walter carefully
introduces himself to Anne Catherick, and reminds her of their
previous encounter. She is shocked but recovers. Her cleaning the
grave is an act of gratitude to the late Mrs Fairlie. Walter notes the
striking similarity between Laura and Anne Catherick. Anne reveals
that she and her mother do not get on well. Walter reassures her that
she does not belong in an asylum and gently informs her that he knows
she wrote 'the letter' to Laura. Again Anne is frightened, then com-
forted, but it is the mention of Sir Percival Glyde which causes her
to scream and to bring her friend Mrs Clements running. Walter is
certain Sir Percival is responsible for Anne's imprisonment but this

interview has been inconclusive. Anne kisses the marble cross on the grave before leaving.

CHAPTER XIII, *pp. 131–8*

Walter brings Marian up to date and they decide to visit Anne Catherick at Todd's Corner farm. Grudgingly Mr Fairlie releases Walter a month early.

Marian discovers Anne and Mrs Clements have left the farm that morning. Anne has suffered a second attack of faintness. Her first had come on while reading about Laura's engagement to Sir Percival in the local paper; her second, it transpires, on hearing of his imminent arrival at Limmeridge. Marian assures Walter that Sir Percival will have to explain everything to her and Mr Gilmore the solicitor if he is to marry Laura.

CHAPTER XIV, *pp. 138–49*

Mr Gilmore arrives and Walter gives him cautious approval. Walter retraces the steps of his walks with Laura, conscious of his present unhappiness. Mr Gilmore has forwarded a copy of the anonymous letter to Sir Percival's solicitor and sent a servant to trace Anne and Mrs Clements. He is confident Sir Percival will be proved honest and honourable. Walter persists in his doubts and decides to leave immediately. Marian insists that he stays and the pattern of their old evenings together is repeated (see Chapter VII) with the addition of Mr Gilmore. Laura reveals some of her feelings for Walter in her piano–playing, which is unusually tense, and some of them in words. Next morning Walter bids farewell to Marian as brother to sister. Laura brings a gift, her sketch of the summerhouse where they first met. Tears overcome them both and a deeply unhappy Laura pleads 'For God's sake, leave me!'

The story continued by Vincent Gilmore (of Chancery Lane, solicitor)

CHAPTER I, *pp. 150–59*

Mr Gilmore picks up the thread of the story from the moment of his arrival at Limmeridge. He records his observations on Mr Fairlie whom he finds unchanged in all his affectations. Laura is 'not looking well', Walter is 'a modest and gentlemanlike man', and the house and estates 'not what they used to be'. Sir Percival arrives on Monday and Mr Gilmore is favourably impressed, particularly as Sir Percival raises the subject of the letter himself. He explains that Anne Catherick was placed in an asylum with her mother's approval and at his own expense, and as a consequence Anne bears a grudge against him. Sir Percival invites – almost challenges – Marian to write to Mrs Catherick to corroborate his story, which she does. Sir Percival asks if Anne saw either Laura or Marian, and where she has been staying, then retires to his room. Marian confides her anxiety to Mr Gilmore and he, having a high regard for her, goes out for a walk slightly more troubled and less confident than before.

CHAPTER II, *pp. 159–69*

At dinner Sir Percival is boisterous and Laura clearly unhappy. Mrs Catherick's reply to Marian's letter arrives, confirming all that Sir Percival has said.

Laura wants to delay the wedding until the end of the year and Marian tells Mr Gilmore she 'cannot and will not accept the responsibility of persuading Laura to marriage'. Mr Gilmore visits Laura, who has been keeping to her room and avoiding Sir Percival, and tries to explain the details of the marriage settlement. Laura insists Marian should continue to live with her after she is married and that she intends to leave everything to her, with a veiled hint (to Mr Gilmore, not the reader) that Walter should receive something. Laura invites Mr Gilmore back, and Sir Percival asks him to visit him at home; he leaves for London, still harbouring some misgivings about the latter and with the settlement not yet fixed.

CHAPTER III, *pp. 169–79*

Eight days later Mr Gilmore is informed the marriage is to take place before the end of the year. He explains the details of the settlement and the family history behind it. Two crucial sums of money are involved: (1) £10,000, which Mme Fosco, Laura's aunt, would receive if Laura died before her; (2) £20,000, which Sir Percival's solicitor maintains Sir Percival should receive if Laura died before him, without any children.

Gilmore takes exception to this, not least because he has discovered that Sir Percival has debts on his estate, and virtually no income. Mr Merriman, Sir Percival's solicitor, arrives to put pressure on Mr Gilmore, who in turn appeals to Mr Fairlie to exercise his influence, but to no avail. It is revealed that Sir Percival is still trying to trace the old woman and Anne Catherick and that a man (Walter) in London is under suspicion and being watched. Mr Gilmore decides to make a final appeal to Mr Fairlie in person and on his way to the station meets a forlorn and haggard Walter, who is about to start a new life abroad.

CHAPTER IV, *pp. 179–84*

Mr Gilmore arrives at Limmeridge and spends an almost sleepless night disturbed by strange cracking and groaning noises and the howling wind, before seeing Mr Fairlie the next morning. He is no more helpful than before, and despite all Mr Gilmore's efforts, refuses to act in Laura's interests. Mr Gilmore states, 'No daughter of mine should have been married to any man alive under such a settlement as I was compelled to make for Laura Fairlie', and repeats it at the end of the chapter.

The story continued by Marian Halcombe (in extracts from her diary)

CHAPTER I, *pp. 184–201*

Laura resolves to tell Sir Percival that she loves another, hoping that this will oblige him to release her from their engagement. Marian doubts the scheme but gains a new respect for Laura's courage. Walter writes to Marian, convinced he is being followed in London and anxious to work abroad (note the use of flashback). Unaware of this, Laura makes her appeal to Sir Percival. He rejects it. In fact, so he maintains, her behaviour has enhanced her value in his eyes. Despite her assurance that she can never love him, Sir Percival goes to Hampshire to prepare for the arrival of his bride. Marian decides to take Laura to her Yorkshire friends, the Arnolds, for a holiday and receives a letter from Walter. He has been appointed draughtsman to an archaeological expedition in Central America, thanks to Marian's recommendations and connections. After a week in Yorkshire, Mr Fairlie recalls Laura and Marian to Limmeridge. The day for the marriage has been fixed, suspects Marian.

CHAPTER II, *pp. 201–17*

The marriage date is fixed for 22 December – even the 'dulled' Laura is stunned by its suddenness. Marian burns Walter's last letter, for safety, and keeps his journey to Honduras a secret from Laura. Laura begs Marian to keep her marriage a secret from Walter. Sir Percival's home is being renovated, so a winter tour of Italy is planned for him and Laura alone, after the wedding. In Rome they will meet Count Fosco and his wife: he is a friend of Sir Percival's, she is a relative of Laura's. Sir Percival accepts Marian's proposal that she continue to live with them on their return. Marian has pangs of conscience over her portrayal of Sir Percival, fearing that she has misjudged him, but she eventually declares 'I hate him' (p. 214). The wedding preparations continue inexorably, with Laura and Marian becoming more distraught as the days go by. The morning of 22 December is wild and unsettled, and 'At eleven o'clock it is all over. They are married.' Marian is overcome by tears.

The Second Epoch

The story continued by Marian Halcombe

CHAPTER I, *pp. 219–33*

Marian is at Blackwater Park awaiting the return of Laura and Sir Percival from Italy, accompanied by the Foscos, who are going to be guests for the summer. She has received a letter from Walter: he is more cheerful, but now beyond communication in a primeval forest. Of Anne Catherick and Mrs Clements there is no news. Mr Gilmore, ill through overwork, is in Germany recuperating and has handed over Fairlie family affairs to his partner, at least temporarily. Mrs Vesey has moved to Clapham to live with her unmarried sister. Mr Fairlie, happy to be alone at last, is occupied having his complete collection photographed.

Laura's letters avoid mentioning her relationship with Sir Percival and Marian fears the worst. Count Fosco puzzles Laura, though his wife has changed for the better. Marian explores the house and grounds and finds them depressing and much inferior to Limmeridge. At the lakeside boathouse she finds a wounded spaniel, apparently shot by the gamekeeper, Baxter. The dog is identified by the housekeeper as Mrs Catherick's. She has been asking for news of her daughter, who has been sighted in the area. Mrs Catherick begs the housekeeper to keep this visit a secret from Sir Percival. As they speak, the dog dies.

CHAPTER II, *pp. 233–47*

Laura returns, unwilling to talk of her marriage at all and, in Marian's eyes, less beautiful than she was. She asks after Walter, but Marian decides to tell her nothing, as before. Sir Percival's manner towards Marian is now less polite and his mood even more irritable. Mme Fosco has indeed changed. She now sits like a statue forever rolling cigarettes for the Count, about whom she is fiercely possessive – Marian suspects something dangerous is suppressed in her behaviour. Marian finds Count Fosco at first fascinating, then admirable. He is fat, and resembles Napoleon; his grey eyes have a hypnotic hold over her. His eccentricities – the garish waistcoats, the menagerie of animals – seem to enhance and not detract from his charm as a companion. His style is unique and overwhelming and Marian notes that Sir Percival is obviously afraid of him. Mr Merriman, Sir Percival's solicitor, arrives unexpectedly.

CHAPTER III, *pp. 248–64*

Marian overhears the conversation between Sir Percival and Mr Merriman. Sir Percival has a 'serious money embarrassment' and his 'relief from it depended upon Laura'. Laura tells Marian that she will help her husband so far as honesty will allow. Next day Sir Percival announces he wishes to see everybody in the library, only to postpone the arrangement in favour of a group walk to the lake. Once there he remarks that 'it looks just the place for a murder, doesn't it?' Fosco disagrees and chillingly explains why not. He then expands on the theme of 'successful' crime: only the crimes committed by the ignorant are detected, not those of wise men. His cynicism annoys both Laura and Marian. Fosco notices traces of blood from the dead spaniel on the ground. Marian reveals Mrs Catherick's visit to Blackwater. The more he hears, the more angry Sir Percival becomes and Fosco intervenes to calm him down. While Sir Percival questions the housekeeper, Fosco extracts from Marian details about Mrs Catherick, her visit, and her daughter, and is clearly surprised by what he learns. Sir Percival is about to leave, almost certainly for Welmingham, when he calls Laura to the library for 'her signature, nothing more', with the Foscos to act as witnesses.

CHAPTER IV, *pp. 264–78*

Marian is asked to act as a witness as Fosco feels it unwise for his own and his wife's signature to be on the document. Laura, however, refuses to sign until she knows the contents of the document, and so does Marian. Once again Sir Percival becomes angry and, despite Fosco's efforts to calm him, insults Laura and leaves with a threat. Laura confides in Marian the misery of her marriage and is almost ready to comply with Sir Percival's wishes, but Marian insists 'We must do what we can to help ourselves.' Marian knows that Sir Percival's previous good behaviour was an act, and she now doubts Fosco. Laura and Marian decide to write to Mr Gilmore's partner, Mr Kyrle, for advice. After putting the letter into the postbag, Marian is whisked away for a half-hour walk by Mme Fosco, who displays a rare friendliness. When she returns, Marian sees Count Fosco putting a letter into the postbag, and deciding to check her own letter finds the envelope is no longer sealed.

CHAPTER V, *pp. 278–88*

At dinner Count Fosco entertains the party with his conversation. Afterwards Laura and Marian take a walk to the lake by themselves.

Laura reveals more of the torment of her marriage, and of Sir Percival's cruelty, and how in Italy he discovered the name of the man she loves, Walter Hartright – 'You shall repent it, and he shall repent it,' he vows. They see a slowly moving figure in the distance, probably a woman, and hurrying home are sure they have been followed. Marian establishes that the figure could not have been the Count, his wife or any of the servants.

CHAPTER VI, *pp. 288–310*

Laura has lost a brooch given her by Marian, and goes into the grounds to search for it. At the lodge gates Marian receives a reply from Mr Kyrle – he suggests Sir Percival's document be shown to him before Laura signs it. As Marian dismisses the messenger, Fosco surprises her: she guesses he knows what has happened. Walking back to the house together, they meet the recently returned Sir Percival. Once Fosco has spoken to him he postpones the signing.

That afternoon Marian has a strange dream involving Walter, his survival of many dangers, and his final return. She is woken by Laura; the brooch has been found by Anne Catherick, whom she has met and spoken to in the park. Anne was the figure they had seen – she still dresses in white. Laura notices their resemblance to each other. Anne has been waiting for days to speak to her alone. She feels guilty that she did not prevent the marriage. Sir Percival no longers frightens her: she is near to death and desires only to be reunited with Mrs Fairlie. Anne knows 'the secret' which will frighten and threaten Sir Percival but, convinced they are being watched, she leaves before explaining it. They arrange to meet at the same time tomorrow.

Sir Percival and the Count have been out walking together, which is unusual. Once they are inside, their moods alter and a change in the weather hints at further developments in the plot.

CHAPTER VII, *pp. 310–25*

Heavy rain falls until midday, though it does not deter Sir Percival
from walking outside. Laura leaves the lunch table to keep her appointment with Anne Catherick. Marian follows later, to avoid causing
suspicion. Reaching the boathouse she finds no sign of Laura or Anne,
only the footprints of a man and a woman, which lead her through the
woods back to the house. Mrs Michelson informs Marian that Laura
has been confined to her room by Sir Percival, and her maid Fanny
dismissed. Angrily Marian demands of Sir Percival that he release
Laura and finds an unexpected – if worrying – ally in Mme Fosco.
Under pressure from these two and the Count, Sir Percival relents.

Marian visits Laura: the meeting with Anne had not taken place.
Early that morning Anne had left a note for Laura at the boathouse.
The Count had spied on their first meeting and then followed Anne,
who escaped him. Sir Percival had waited for Laura at the boathouse.
He snatched the note, which he had already read, from her and then
interrogated her. Insisting that she was still withholding information,
he had imprisoned her. Marian decides to write to Mr Kyrle and Mr
Fairlie, using Fanny as a safe messenger.

CHAPTER VIII, *pp. 325–38*

Marian suspects her writing materials may have been tampered with
while she talked with Laura. Once downstairs, the Count continues
to pay Marian compliments, which angers and annoys Mme Fosco.
Marian returns to her room to write the letters to Mr Kyrle and Mr
Fairlie, and then visits Laura. Laura is sure they are being spied on
– Marian suspects Mme Fosco. Marian takes the letters to the village
inn where Fanny is staying. Fanny will post Mr Kyrle's in London,
Mr Fairlie's she will deliver by hand to Limmeridge. Marian fears
she may have been followed on her journey. Meanwhile Sir Percival
has threatened Laura again.

At dinner the Count is hot and flushed, and Marian wonders if he has been out. Afterwards he asks provokingly if she has anything for the postbag, before playing the piano, singing and giving his opinion on 'national' music. Marian eventually returns to Laura, to talk and complete her journal.

CHAPTER IX, *pp. 338–56*

Unable to concentrate on her journal Marian leans out of her window and hears the Count and Sir Percival, who are about to continue their conversation in the library. Marian is determined, for Laura's sake, to overhear them and creeps round the outside of the house before perching between the flowerpots on the verandah above the open windows. She discovers that:

1. the Count and Sir Percival both face financial ruin;
2. her second letter to Mr Kyrle is known about;
3. the Count, as the cleverer partner, now insists on controlling plans;
4. as the Count reveals, Sir Percival would receive £20,000 and Mme Fosco £10,000 were Laura to die childless.

The Count puts pressure on Sir Percival to reveal 'the secret' but Sir Percival will only acknowledge that Anne Catherick is vital to it and that her discovery is crucial. Fosco promises his help and, hearing that Anne looks like Laura, leaves in a cheerful mood. Marian, who has been drenched by the rain, returns to her room.

CHAPTER X, *pp. 356–78*

Marian records all that she's heard in her journal, but she is now suffering from fever as a result of her soaking, and her final entry becomes incoherent. There follows a 'Postscript by a Sincere Friend', i.e. Count Fosco, who adds a note of admiration for Marian in his own florid style.

The story continued by Frederick Fairlie Esq. of Limmeridge House

... it is told under duress, and not without considerable complaint.

Fanny, Laura's maid, has arrived at Limmeridge, bringing Marian's letter. At the village inn she had been visited by Mme Fosco – ostensibly with more (unspecified) messages from Marian. Five minutes after drinking the tea Mme Fosco had prepared Fanny had fainted. She recovered to find her letters had been interfered with.

Marian's letter, suggesting Laura take refuge at Limmeridge, upsets and threatens Mr Fairlie. He replies by suggesting that Marian comes first on her own to discuss matters with him. Meanwhile a worried Mr Kyrle has written to Mr Fairlie describing the envelope he has received, with Marian's handwriting on it, which contained only a blank sheet of paper.

Count Fosco, not Marian, calls on Mr Fairlie. He charms Mr Fairlie – at first – and reports Marian's illness and the disagreement between Sir Percival and Laura. He suggests Laura be invited to Limmeridge immediately, even as Marian recovers. Fosco will arrange for Laura to break her journey at his London house in St John's Wood, before putting her on the train himself to Cumberland. Mr Fairlie writes a letter of invitation to Laura, secretly confident that his peace will not be disturbed: he is sure Laura would not leave Blackwater without Marian.

The story continued by Eliza Michelson (housekeeper at Blackwater Park)

CHAPTER I, *pp. 379–97*

Mrs Michelson describes Marian's fever and how she refuses to take Fosco's mixture. The Count and Mr Dawson, the blunt-mannered local doctor, disagree on medical matters throughout the chapter. Marian is nursed by Mme Fosco and Mrs Michelson. Laura stays up with her sister, but she is no real help as a nurse. Fosco arranges for a nurse to come from London, though he knows Mr Dawson will be suspicious. The nurse, Mrs Rubelle, is dark, foreign and silent, but as far as Mrs Michelson can see she is good at her job. Marian improves while Fosco is in London, but then has a relapse and a London physician is summoned. Fosco identifies the fever as typhus, but Mr Dawson denies it. Laura tries to enter the room, though strictly forbidden to do so, and faints. The London doctor confirms Fosco's diagnosis. After ten anxious days Marian improves, but Laura declines. At the same time the Count and Mr Dawson fall out for the final time, and Mr Dawson departs, leaving Blackwater Park with two patients and no doctor. Sir Percival tells Mrs Michelson that he himself plans to leave Blackwater as an economy measure, dismissing all the staff except herself and the foolish Margaret Porcher.

CHAPTER II, *pp. 397–419*

Mrs Michelson is sent to Torquay to find lodgings so Marian and Laura can convalesce there, before they return to Limmeridge. The restrictions imposed by Sir Percival, however, make this an impossible mission. She returns to find the Foscos have gone to London, apparently taking Marian, and without informing Laura. Laura is greatly distressed despite Sir Percival's assurance that Marian is on her way to Limmeridge, and decides to follow her to London. Sir Percival arranges for Fosco to meet Laura at the station the following day. Laura writes to Mrs Vesey asking to stay, as she dislikes the prospect of a night under Fosco's roof. Her parting from Sir Percival appears to be a final one.

Mrs Michelson sees Mrs Rubelle in the garden and discovers from her that Marian has not left at all. Mrs Michelson offers her resignation immediately, shocked by Sir Percival's lies and deceptions, and by his erratic behaviour. Mrs Rubelle leaves, however, and Mrs Michelson consents to look after Marian, taking the precaution of making the gardener come in for the night. It is a wise move as Sir Percival behaves wildly, jumps into the chaise, rides to a local inn and leaves on the morning train – destination unknown. Mrs Michelson and

Marian leave Blackwater at the same time, the latter on her way to Limmeridge. Unfortunately, Mrs Michelson cannot remember the exact date of Laura's departure.

The story continued in several narratives

1. The narrative of Hester Pinhorn (cook in the service of Count Fosco), pp. 420–25
Hester, the Fosco's cook in St John's Wood, gives a description of Lady Glyde's arrival there: she is very ill, as the doctor confirms, possibly with heart disease. Next day she appears to make a recovery, only to collapse and die in the evening. The doctor registers the death himself, which is unusual. Hester concludes by stating that Fosco was never alone with Lady Glyde or seen to give her any medicine.

2. The narrative of the doctor, pp. 425–6
The doctor, Alfred Goodricke, confirms that she died on 25 July at No. 5 Forest Road, St John's Wood, and that the cause of her death was an aneurism (a form of heart disease).

3. The narrative of Jane Gould, p. 426
She prepared the body for the coffin and saw the coffin lid screwed down.

4. The narrative of the tombstone, p. 426
Confirming details of 'Laura's' birth, marriage and death.

5. The narrative of Walter Hartright, pp. 426–31
Walter reaches London in the autumn of 1850, having survived death by disease and at the hands of the Indians, and drowning (as prefigured in Marian's dream). He visits his mother and sister in Hampstead and learns of 'Laura's' death. He travels to 'Laura's' grave at Limmeridge. At sunset he sees two women approaching the grave: one is Marian; the other, unbelievably, Laura.

The Third Epoch

The story continued by Walter Hartright

CHAPTER I, *pp. 433–5*

A week later. Walter is living in London, under an assumed name, with his two 'sisters' sharing the apartment below (note how this relationship fulfils the promises made on p. 148). All three are poverty-stricken; but Walter is nevertheless determined to fight Laura's battle.

CHAPTER II, *pp. 435–51*

Walter tells Marian's story first: Marian was informed of Laura's sudden death by Mrs Michelson at Blackwater. It was three weeks before she was fit to visit London and consult Mr Kyrle. She was convinced that foul play was involved. Mr Kyrle, however, found Fosco co-operative with his inquiries and could find no evidence to support her charge. Marian returned to Limmeridge.

Mr Fairlie had been warned by Fosco that Anne Catherick, now back in the asylum, was suffering under the delusion that she was Lady Glyde. Marian visited the asylum and discovered it was Laura who had been imprisoned. By bribing her nurse with a large sum of money, Marian secured Laura's release.

Laura had been met at the station by Fosco and then taken to a strange house, where she had obviously been drugged. Her recollections are vague but include being attended by Mrs Rubelle, and taking a carriage journey with Fosco, eventually finding herself in the asylum with the new identity of Anne Catherick.

Back at Limmeridge, Mr Fairlie refused to recognize his niece, and with the asylum authorities in pursuit Laura was no longer safe at their former home. Marian decided to return to the comparative safety of a large city, London. They stopped at the Limmeridge graveyard on their way, meeting Walter there by chance and so changing the course of their lives.

CHAPTER III, *pp. 451–9*

In London, Walter takes a poorly paid but anonymous job as an engraver, while Marian is housekeeper. They pool their resources (which amount to a little more than £400) as a fund for Laura, and to finance their attempts to redress 'an infamous wrong'. Laura has indeed suffered and her resemblance to Anne Catherick is now uncanny. Slowly she is nursed into better health by Walter and Marian, whose devotion is faultless. Walter is well aware of the danger from Sir Percival and urges special caution to Marian as he leaves to see Mr Kyrle with all the evidence so far gathered.

CHAPTER IV, *pp. 460–71*

Walter visits Mr Kyrle in his office, and immediately regrets not having arranged a different rendezvous, as he fears he may be followed. Mr Kyrle is not encouraging: the facts will be difficult to refute, the process extremely expensive, and the outcome uncertain. Walter must take the law into his own hands. Mr Kyrle has a sealed letter for Marian, which Walter takes with him. His premonition is confirmed, and he is followed, but he manages to escape his pursuers and reach home. Marian's letter is from Fosco, carrying compliments to her and threats to Walter, which they both ignore. He decides to visit Blackwater: (1) to establish the date of Laura's journey to London – the weakest link in the chain of evidence; (2) to uncover 'the secret' which frightens Sir Percival so much.

CHAPTER V, *pp. 471–8*

Walter's visit to Blackwater proves fruitless. Neither Mr Dawson, nor Margaret Porcher, nor the gardener are of any help and the inn at which Sir Percival had stopped has been boarded up. At the Park he meets a suspicious lawyer's clerk who tries, unsuccessfully, to provoke an argument.

Back home, Marian fills Walter in on Sir Percival's family history. They decide to trace Mrs Clements as a means of revealing 'the secret' and find out she is now living in London. Walter wastes no time in visiting her.

CHAPTER VI, *pp. 478–85*

Mrs Clements lives near Gray's Inn Road. She describes how she and Anne Catherick had travelled from Todd's Corner to London and then to Grimsby, where Anne had become very ill with heart disease. Despite this Anne was determined to meet Lady Glyde in private again, and they travelled to Sandon, four miles from Blackwater, together. After one of her meetings with Laura, Anne had become ill again. Mrs Clements had gone to the boathouse instead and met not Laura, but Fosco. He had delivered a message purportedly from Laura, advising them to go to London, where they would all meet soon. The Count had given Anne some treatment and she seemed to make a spectacular recovery. Once they were in London they had tried to contact Laura but with no success, until an elderly lady (Mme Fosco) called with a message from her. Mrs Clements had left with the lady in a cab, and had been abandoned in mid-journey. On returning to their lodgings she had found no sign of Anne; nor had she been returned to the asylum.

CHAPTER VII, *pp. 485–98*

Walter is told the story of Mrs Catherick: her unexpected marriage
to a man she had spurned for so long; her alleged affair with Sir
Percival; the showdown between her husband and Sir Percival (which
had led to Catherick's emigration to America); and, finally, her denial
of the allegation and her attempt to establish a respectable life in
Welmingham – probably supported by Sir Percival. Walter is sure
'the secret' involves all these elements, and yet is somehow concealed
by them. The identity of Anne's father is still a mystery: she resembles
neither her mother nor Sir Percival. Walter tells Mrs Clements of
Anne's death and asks for Mrs Catherick's address. With foreboding,
and a warning, Mrs Clements gives it to him.

CHAPTER VIII, *pp. 498–511*

Laura's recovery is helped by an innocent deception of Walter's: he
makes out that her drawings have been sold, when in fact the only
buyer is himself.

Walter visits Mrs Catherick. She is unwelcoming, cold and apparently unconcerned by her daughter's death. At the mention of Old
Welmingham and her husband she flushes, but regains her composure
and launches into a vigorous defence of her character and behaviour
since then. Walter shakes her again by declaring he is sure Sir Percival
is not Anne's father as is commonly supposed, but Mrs Catherick will
reveal no more, nor will she incriminate Sir Percival. (See p. 503 for
a rare example of Collins making a direct social comment.)

CHAPTER IX, *pp. 511–23*

Walter sees the lawyer's clerk, who had tried to pick a quarrel with
him once before, emerging from the house next to Mrs Catherick's

– obviously he is still being followed. Reflecting on his interview with Mrs Catherick, Walter identifies two crucial items: (1) The vestry at Old Welmingham, (2) Sir Percival's mother: why had Mrs Catherick been so contemptuous of her? He goes to Old Welmingham Church, noticing two 'spies' in the churchyard. The vestry clerk eventually shows him the marriage register. He reveals that a duplicate is kept by the former vestry clerk, a solicitor in nearby Knowlesbury. Walter finds the record of Sir Percival's father's marriage: the only notable feature is that it appears squeezed on to the bottom of the page. Walter decides to visit the solicitor's office and sets off walking the five miles to Knowlesbury, well aware he is being followed.

CHAPTER X, *pp. 524–41*

On his way to Knowlesbury, Walter is trapped into making an assault on his two followers, who charge him before the local magistrate. Walter is remanded in custody for three days – a ploy of Sir Percival's to gain time and freedom from Walter's interference. Walter, however, uses Mr Dawson the surgeon to stand bail and is freed that afternoon.

Once in the solicitor's office, Walter examines the duplicate register. There is no record of Sir Felix Glyde's marriage: 'the secret' is out. Sir Percival is illegitimate and has no claim to his title, and the parish records of Old Welmingham have been falsified.

The Old Welmingham vestry is his next destination and once again he is pursued, this time by three men whom he eventually outruns. Walter meets the anxious parish clerk: the vestry keys are missing, and when they go to investigate, the vestry is on fire. Inside is Sir Percival who, despite all Walter's efforts, dies in the blaze. The records, too, are burnt.

CHAPTER XI, *pp. 541–48*

Walter receives a letter from Marian saying that all is well, and he replies at length. At the inquest Sir Percival's identity is confirmed, but no progress is made on his motive for being in the vestry, for Walter keeps his suspicions quiet. Visiting the scene of the fire he is struck by the sudden transformation of the place. Back at his hotel he receives a letter from Mrs Catherick.

The story continued by Mrs Catherick, pp. 548–60

Mrs Catherick recounts the story of Sir Percival's courtship of her – how he bought her gifts and how his purpose was to obtain the vestry keys. Mrs Catherick obliged him, but also watched him, thus learning the secret of his illegitimacy and the false entry in the register. Sir Percival refused to clear her name, but agreed to pay her 'a handsome yearly allowance', provided she kept quiet and remained in Welmingham. She confirms the reasons for Anne's wearing white, and tells how Anne had accidentally picked up 'the secret' and discovered its power over Sir Percival, without knowing the details. Sir Percival had insisted Anne be put in an asylum, and Mrs Catherick had consented: after all, her desire to be socially respectable in Welmingham would be made easier.

The story continued by Walter Hartright

CHAPTER I, *pp. 560–64*

Walter receives a letter from Marian saying that she and Laura have moved to Fulham; Walter senses the influence of Fosco. Sir Percival's estate is left to its original and rightful heir, and Walter decides to keep Sir Percival's fraud a secret, as no useful purpose would be served by revealing it now. Walter then takes the train to London.

CHAPTER II, *pp. 564–76*

In Fulham, Marian tells him she has seen Fosco and the asylum owner outside in the street. Without revealing anything to Laura, Marian had met Fosco who confirmed his wish to put Laura back in the asylum, expressed his continued admiration for Marian, and passed on a warning to Walter to avoid confronting him.

Walter is undeterred by the threat. He insists Laura is told of Sir Percival's death, and Marian does so. Walter tries to establish the identity of Anne Catherick's father: his search leads him to the conclusion it was Philip Fairlie, hence her strong resemblance to Laura.

CHAPTER III, *pp. 576–82*

Both Marian and Laura recover their health. Unfortunately, Walter's feelings of awkwardness return simultaneously. He consults Marian about the future and they decide not to return to Limmeridge. With Marian's blessing, Walter and Laura are married.

CHAPTER IV, *pp. 582–8*

They return to London. Walter is convinced that Fosco is a spy and having observed him closely in St John's Wood, decides to follow him to the opera – accompanied by his old friend Pesca.

CHAPTER V, *pp. 588–98*

At the opera Pesca does not recognize Fosco, but Fosco recognizes and clearly fears him. Furthermore, a man with a scar on his left cheek pursues Fosco from the theatre at the interval. Pesca reluctantly reveals his secret to Walter: his membership of the Brotherhood, a secret political society, its complete control over his life, and its secret identification mark, which is branded on the arm. Fosco, it seems, is also a member and one who, as Walter knows, has been false to its aims.

CHAPTER VI, *pp. 598–605*

Despite the risks, Walter is determined to pursue the Count, and as a precaution he writes a letter to Pesca identifying the Count as a member false to the Brotherhood, sending it inside a sealed envelope with the instruction that it should not be opened before next morning. He tells Marian of his purpose, leaves her to guard Laura and takes a cab to St John's Wood. Once there he sees the man with a scar again – is he still pursuing Fosco? Finally he is admitted to the house.

CHAPTER VII, *pp. 605–18*

Fosco is packing and about to leave. Walter's arrival is an inconvenience, and he is tempted to consider murder. Walter warns Fosco of the precaution he has taken with the sealed letter, and demands a signed confession of the conspiracy as well as proof of the date on which Laura travelled to London (a date which Walter is certain will prove to be later than the one on the doctor's certificate of death). Fosco is prepared to meet these demands provided he and his wife are allowed free passage from London, and that he may challenge Walter to a duel at a later date. Walter agrees, and Fosco calmly writes his confession. That done he leaves his birds to the London Zoo, but not his mice – he cannot bear to be parted from them. He burns the sealed letter which has been retrieved before nine o'clock from Pesca, and leaves in a cab. Another cab follows him, and inside it is the man with the scar.

The story continued by Isidor, Ottavio, Baldassare Fosco, pp. 618–32

The list of absurd titles which follow this heading is intended to be satirical of Fosco and his enormous vanity.

Fosco, in his own inimitable and flamboyant style, covers the ground which Walter has already shown the reader. He confirms all of Walter's theories and suspicions and declares his passionate love for Marian, which he also acknowledges as his only weakness. The whole account is characterized by his usual insistence on his own ingenuity, intelligence and flair. He concludes by asserting his innocence.

The story concluded by Walter Hartright

CHAPTER I, *pp. 633–40*

Walter gathers the third and clinching piece of evidence, the entry in the livery stables' order book dated 26 July: 'Brougham to Count Fosco, 5 Forest Road. Two o'clock ...' Having told Mr Kyrle, he, Marian, Laura and the coach-driver all travel to Limmeridge. Mr Fairlie is finally persuaded, as are the tenants, that his niece is alive, and the inscription on the grave is corrected to record Anne Catherick's death. Walter, Laura and Marian return to London.

CHAPTER II, *pp. 640–44*

Walter visits Paris on business, taking Pesca with him in the hope that a holiday will lift the Italian's depression. In their hotel Pesca is questioned by the man with a scar on his cheek, who is a member of the Brotherhood and still in pursuit of Fosco. Pesca fears the worst and wishes to leave Paris immediately.

As they approach Notre Dame, they see a great crowd outside the morgue: inside lies the dead Fosco, killed by the Brotherhood, branded a traitor, but still admired by the French women. His disguise as a French artisan had not saved him. Mme Fosco survives him, living in Versailles, writing her husband's biography and tending his grave.

CHAPTER III, *pp. 644–6*

Walter and Laura's first child, a boy christened Walter, is born. While Walter is working in Ireland, Laura, Marian and the baby travel to Limmeridge and only when he arrives does Walter discover why: Mr Fairlie has died and their early happy days at Limmeridge can be re-created at last. Walter's son is now heir to the estate.

Characters

WALTER HARTRIGHT

Walter is the hero of the story and one of its chief narrators. It is as a result of his efforts that the mystery of the woman in white can be revealed and the schemes of the Count and Sir Percival be exposed. The narrative scheme is organized and controlled by him – only after he has gathered the various strands of the narrative from Mr Gilmore, Marian Halcombe, Mr Fairlie, Mrs Catherick and others, then added them to his own, and arranged them in chronological order can the story be told as if it were a hearing in court (see p. 33), with the reader in the role of jury member and Judge.

For the most part Walter's narrative shows qualities of succinctness, precision and accuracy. It is less impassioned than the Count's, although there are moments which stand out: Pesca's excitement amid the broken teacups, to the dismay of Walter's sister Sarah (p. 38); the introduction of Marian with its extraordinary and brilliant use of anti-climax (p. 58); the gentle irony of his treatment of Mrs Vesey (p. 72); his own sense of desolation during his last moments at Limmeridge (pp. 147–9), the confrontation with Count Fosco (pp. 605–18); the deaths of Sir Percival (pp. 537–41) and Fosco (pp. 642–4) – all these are high points in the novel.

Not only does Walter carry a large portion of the narrative (pp. 33–149, 426–31, and almost all of the Third Epoch), he also provides, with Marian, its moral centre. His surname Hartright (i.e. 'heartright', or true) is no accident. (Dickens, Collins's friend and collaborator, often gave his characters names which indicated their key qualities – Gradgrind and Bounderby, for example, in *Hard Times* (1854).) Walter's heart is true and faithful; and when he realizes his love for Laura, he is prepared to undergo considerable suffering

(p. 178) and hardship before eventually achieving his prize, like a knight in medieval romance. His love for Laura is the motivation for nearly all his actions, including his exile in Central America, and it inspires him to challenge and defy Sir Percival and Count Fosco. His exploits are an exhibition of the Latin motto *Omnia vincit amor* – love conquers all things. Walter's love is quite different from the financial motives of Sir Percival and Count Fosco: '"There shall be no money motive," I said, "No idea of personal advantage in the service I mean to render to Lady Glyde"' (p. 465).

Walter's credentials as a hero are established before he meets Laura, in several telling ways. His rescue of Pesca from drowning (p. 36) immediately shows his physical courage and loyalty to a friend. His devotion to his mother and sister is praiseworthy and underlines his attachment to family life. His treatment of Anne Catherick, the woman in white, when they first meet at the Hampstead crossroads is sympathetic, kindly and considerate – qualities which he displays before almost everybody he meets, including the vegetable-like Mrs Vesey. It is his conduct towards Anne which impresses Marian: '"I was predisposed in your favour when you first told me of your conduct towards that unhappy woman whom you met under such remarkable circumstances"' (p. 94). It is his friendship with Marian which creates an alliance strong enough to defeat Sir Percival and drive Count Fosco to France. Even in his dealings with the provoking Mr Fairlie, Walter manages to retain his dignity.

In addition to these qualities, Walter has ingenuity and, at the critical stage of his tussle with Fosco, a clear tactical brain. This is shown, for example, by his decision to hide Laura in an obscure part of London, and by the sealed letter which he sends to Pesca, identifying Fosco as a member of the Brotherhood – a move which elicits a compliment from the Count: '"But I am a just man even to my enemy, and I will acknowledge ... that they are cleverer brains than I thought them"' (p. 608). Lastly, Walter Hartright is a talented artist and drawing master. He appreciates beauty in human form (Laura), in landscape (at Limmeridge), in moral purity (Marian). He is a good teacher: '... but the best of all, the most intelligent and the most attentive, was a Mr Hartright ... modest and gentlemanlike' (p. 283); and of all the characters in the novel he is the most appropriate master of Limmeridge and its artistic treasures.

His values are shared and reinforced by Laura, the gifted musician, and Marian, the gifted writer – Walter junior will be brought up surrounded by enlightened influences.

COUNT FOSCO

(See pp. 239–46 for an extended description of Fosco, by Marian.)

Along with Sir Percival Glyde, Count Fosco is the major villain in the novel: he shares Sir Percival's need for money and shares also a ruthlessness in order to obtain it, but there the similarities end. Sir Percival, after his initial display of courtesy and politeness, is a limited man who becomes the victim of his limitations, whereas Count Fosco is a man of seemingly boundless intellect, subtlety and, paradoxically, charm. With the possible exception of Marian Halcombe, Fosco is Collins's most striking creation in the novel. Every feature of Count Fosco is intriguing, fascinating and unusual. His name, which is almost certainly an alias, is the Italian for dark or dismal, a reflection of his purpose if not of his personality. Perhaps it is a little joke of his own, made at the expense of the ill-educated English; if so, it is quite in keeping with his arrogance and wit. His size, which would appear to be such a handicap, making him conspicuous and clumsy, is in fact accompanied by his distinctive 'noiseless tread', which surprises and frightens Marian on more than one occasion (e.g. pp. 292, 327). His relationship with the servile Mme Fosco, who submits herself entirely to his will and the production of his cigarettes and who, after his death, devotes herself to tending his grave and writing his biography, is set up as a contrast with his love and admiration for the strong-minded and independent Marian. Most readers will share his feelings for Marian and recognize that they have several qualities in common, not least intellect and determination. His pets and his way of speaking to them add a delicious humour and eccentricity to his character and to the novel, a necessary balance to the more serious elements; and his ability to tame the fierce bloodhound (pp. 243–4) makes a neat contrast with Sir Percival's experience with the greyhound Nina (p. 156), as well as being an apt image of his relationship with Sir Percival. Fosco's cool intellect restrains and controls Sir Percival's hot temper and impulsive will in masterly fashion, and reinforces the impression of something other-worldly in Fosco's ability to manipulate the natural world to his own advantage.

There is an intriguing parallel between Fosco and Walter: just as Walter saved Pesca from drowning, so Fosco saved Sir Percival from near-assassination (p. 213). Perhaps in Fosco's case it is a matter of 'honour among thieves', but more likely it is a sign that Collins has created a fully rounded character, and not merely a cardboard cutout villain, as finer feelings are shown not to be the exclusive property of the 'good' characters. In fact Fosco's appreciation of music and fondness for singing are further links with the 'good' characters (Walter, Laura, Marian, Mr Gilmore and Pesca); and it is appropriate, as well as ironic, that it is a visit to the opera, where he naturally becomes the leader of the audience, which provides the crucial link in the chain of events leading to his death (pp. 588–92).

As a man of science, he describes himself to Marian with typically engaging bravado as '"one of the first [i.e. best] experimental chemists living"', and claims to have discovered '"a means of petrifying the body after death, so as to preserve it, as hard as marble, to the end of time"'. He is able to diagnose typhus fever correctly when the local doctor fails to, to revive Anne Catherick for her journey to London, and to prepare a sleeping potion, administered by Mme Fosco, for the dismissed serving maid at the inn. His talents do not stop at being a master of both arts and science; it is his use of the resemblance between Laura and Anne Catherick, which is the linchpin of the plot and the novel. Fosco's ingenuity at this stage is the embodiment of Collins's own, so it is not perhaps surprising that as a character he is given so many varied and memorable characteristics, and that whenever he is present in a scene the reader's interest is heightened and intensified. His appearances are anticipated like the return of a favourite actor to the stage and certainly self-dramatization is one of his many gifts.

Fosco plays a major part in the climax to the novel, the gripping confrontation with Walter (pp. 605–32). His fleet-footed intellect and wit are the perfect foils to Walter's more dogged and resolute qualities, and his sense of style adds an extra ingredient to this fine set piece. His language is highly idiosyncratic (see for example, his entry in Marian's diary, pp. 358–60), and yet it is a forceful expression of his personality, adding colour and vitality to the narrative in the same way as his garish waistcoats enliven the dull drabness of Blackwater Park. Even his fondness for pastry, which may explain his corpulence, is an endearing feature.

All these elements are united by his enormous self-confidence and bravado. Whatever the challenge Fosco appears to be able to meet it, and finally he is the victim, not of another individual's strength or skill, but of the Brotherhood's revenge – an impersonal assassination for an unspecified crime. Even in death he can command the admiration of the French women peering into the morgue: '"Ah, what a handsome man!"' (p. 643). Walter remarks, '"Sincerely as I loathed the man, the prodigious strength of his character, even in its most trivial aspects, impressed me in spite of myself."' As readers, we can afford to be more generous than Fosco's opponent: he is a great fictional creation who sustains our interest in the book and its outcome, and his death signals that the story is nearly at an end. Both Marian (p. 241) and Fosco himself (p. 615) note his resemblance to Napoleon – the comparison is a just one.

MARIAN HALCOMBE

'I am dark and ugly and she is fair and pretty. Everybody thinks me crabbed and odd (with perfect justice); and everybody thinks her sweet-tempered and charming (with more justice still). In short, she is an angel, and I am – Try some of that marmalade, Mr Hartright, and finish the sentence in the name of female propriety, for yourself.' (pp. 60–61)

Marian is speaking to Walter on the morning of his first breakfast at Limmeridge. He is just recovering from the shock of the contrast between the elegance of her form and movement, and the ugliness of her face, when she disarms him with this lively and typical display of intelligence, wit and self-deprecation. She continues to show these qualities throughout the novel, and reveals others later on, not least a physical courage which is the equal of Walter's own.

She is not a typical heroine (Laura is the model), just as Fosco is the antithesis of the lean and hungry villain of Victorian melodrama. It is against the background of Laura's blonde and beautiful passivity that Marian's forceful and vibrant personality can stand out, and like Fosco her character is built upon a contradiction – her facial ugliness is at odds with the beauty of her soul. Indeed Fosco is her counterpart in several ways. They share vitality, strength of character and rare intelligence; moreover they feel a strong fascination for each other, which is allowed to develop for a time, before the demands of the plot take over.

Marian is admired by several of the men in the novel. Mr Gilmore describes her as 'A sensitive, vehement, passionate nature – a woman of ten thousand in these trivial, superficial times' (p. 159). Fosco tells Sir Percival:

'Can you look at Miss Halcombe and not see that she has the foresight and the resolution of a man? With that woman for my friend I would snap these fingers of mine at the world. With that woman for my enemy, I, Fosco, with all my brains and experience – I, Fosco, cunning as the devil himself, as you have told me a hundred times – I walk, in your English phrase, upon egg shells!' (p. 346)

Walter sees her as 'the fearless, noble creature' (p. 148), and at one stage Laura fears that Walter will lose interest in her: '"You will end in liking Marian better than you like me – you will, because I am so helpless"' (p. 499). But Marian's devotion to Laura is constant, the mainspring of all her actions, and the intensity of her feelings for her sister are equalled only by Walter's. '"My sister's future is my dearest care in life,"' she declares (p. 132). Some readers might feel that Walter would gain more from a match with Marian, at least in terms of stimulating company, but this is never really a possibility. Walter's love is blind to the claims of all except Laura, and as it turns out he will always be able to enjoy the companionship of Marian at Limmeridge.

It is Fosco who recognizes Marian's gifts as a writer after he has read her journal, and even allowing for his habitual hyperbole and delight in seeing his own character described, his judgements are fair:

Every page has charmed, refreshed, delighted me ... the wonderful power of memory, the accurate observation of character ... the charming outbursts of womanly feeling ... The presentation of my own character is masterly in the extreme. (pp. 358–9)

Her skill extends to the description of place: her version of Blackwater Park is both detailed and highly impressionistic (pp. 225–7), providing a telling contrast with Walter's in the depiction of Limmeridge. The 'outbursts' mentioned by Fosco are a special feature of her narrative. They give the novel a greater emotional range than it would otherwise have, and they reveal a nature which cannot always control the turbulence of its own moods and emotions. Her famous tirade against men is worth quoting in full:

'Are you to break your heart to set his mind at ease? No man under heaven deserves these sacrifices from us women. Men! They are the enemies of our innocence and our peace – they drag us away from our parents' love and our sisters' friendship – they take us body and soul to themselves, and fasten our helpless lives to theirs as they chain up a dog to his kennel. And what does the best of them give us in return? Let me go, Laura – I'm mad when I think of it!' (p. 203)

It is worth noting that it is the combination of Mr Fairlie and Sir Percival which provokes this outburst, a particularly poisonous pair of the male sex and not perhaps wholly typical of their gender. Some readers have suggested that the tirade can be seen as an early manifesto for the liberation of women – or even as a lesbian battlecry, with Marian revealing a suppressed passion for the beautiful Laura, under stress. Moreover, so the argument goes, Marian's masculine features, and statements like 'If only I had the privileges of a man' (p. 270) and 'If I had been a man, I would have knocked him down' (p. 268), can be adduced as further evidence of her inclinations, and to explain the intensity of her attachment to Laura. This would be to ignore, however, the occasions when Marian behaves in 'womanly' fashion, (for example when she breaks down after her tirade), and to discount other declarations of hers such as 'Any woman who is sure of her own wits is a match at any time for a man who is not sure of his own temper' (p. 332). Those who search for such meanings will find them, but to quote Julian Symons from the introduction to the Penguin edition, 'it is doubtful whether such thoughts were in Collins's mind' (p. 15). It might be suggested that Marian's frustrations are those of a woman whose talents are admired by men, but who is not loved by men – in the opinion of most readers, it is their loss.

Marian's relationship to Walter eventually becomes that of sister to brother, united by their love for Laura and deep respect for each other. Walter confides in her from the beginning, and by revealing his encounter with the woman in white excites Marian's curiosity; this in turn leads to the identification of Anne Catherick – a vital step in uncovering the plot. Marian's kindness is tempered by practicality. She breaks the tension which has marked the later weeks of Walter's first visit to Limmeridge, by taking him into the garden and revealing '"I have discovered your secret"' (p. 98) – his love for Laura – and tells him of Laura's engagement to Sir Percival. She shows him sympathy and understanding, and softens the blow by explaining a plan which will secure his early release from Mr Fairlie's contract. In the same way her treatment of the wounded spaniel is both affectionate and practical. Later her letters to Mr Kyrle, the solicitor, are wise moves in the deadly game with Fosco.

Her courage can best be seen when she listens to the conversation between Sir Percival and Count Fosco, perched precariously on the parapet, steadily being drenched by the rain (pp. 338–56). Back in her room she recalls all the details of the discussion and, before succumbing to the fever, commits them to paper, thus making a record which will prove invaluable to Walter as he assembles the evidence. Tenacity is yet another of her gifts, and it is of great value to her in securing Laura's release from the asylum (pp. 443–5); here she also displays that generosity and indifference to personal wealth which unites all the 'good' characters in the novel.

Marian brings an element of vitality into the novel, as well as passion, wit and courage. She is, like Fosco, an outsize character, and yet a credible and likeable one; without her *The Woman in White* would be not only incomplete and unsatisfying, it would also be unbalanced.

SIR PERCIVAL GLYDE

Collins takes the precaution of introducing Sir Percival to the reader before Count Fosco, so that the baronet is established as a dynamic and impressive force before his partner arrives on the scene and takes over the plot – and indeed much of the reader's interest. This proves to be a wise decision as for the most part Sir Percival is a less fully realized character than Fosco. His behaviour is stereotyped in the mould of the harsh and brutal baronet, beloved of Victorian melodrama, but less admired now. His name may not be as obviously descriptive as some others in the novel, but it is reminiscent of the movement of reptiles and it is a short journey from there to the Garden of Eden. Once the veneer of his deceitful courtship is stripped away, Sir Percival's true features are revealed, but essentially they do not develop. On his first entry, Sir Percival manages to make a favourable impression upon Mr Gilmore, whose natural caution is a handicap on this occasion: "'I found him to be a most prepossessing man, so far as manners and appearance were concerned'" (p. 152). Even Marian is prepared to admit, 'There can be no doubt that Laura's future husband is a very handsome man' (p. 210). This is a good example of Collins's use of the device of contradiction: Sir Percival's handsome outside conceals an evil disposition; while with Marian it is the reverse.

The only clues to Sir Percival's true nature before his marriage to Laura, are Anne Catherick's comments to Walter at their first encounter (pp. 51–2), which may not yet be associated with Sir Percival. His 'dry, sharp cough', too, is a well-judged detail in his characterization, as it becomes more troublesome and insistent as his desperation increases (pp. 189, 215). It is on his return from honeymoon that his plot to secure £20,000 from Laura's inheritance is set in motion. Laura's honesty and innocence fail to move him, and he declares '"I believe in nothing about her, but her money"' (p. 355). Once he meets resistance from his bride in the matter of the signature, his already injured pride inflames his violent temper, and from that moment he barely keeps it under control. The irritability which Mr Gilmore had remarked and dismissed (p. 156) now dominates his behaviour. It appears not just in his treatment of Laura, in his willingness to imprison her under the vile guard Margaret Porcher, but in his treatment of animals and the natural world, and in this he differs totally from Fosco. Mrs Michelson describes his approach at one point:

He came towards us, slashing viciously at the flowers with his riding whip. When he was near enough to see my face he stopped, struck at his boot with the whip, and burst out laughing, so harshly and violently that the birds flew away, startled, from the tree by which he stood. (p. 412)

She also describes his night-time departure from Blackwater, 'lashing the horse into a gallop' (p. 417).

Sir Percival's primary concern is to conceal his secret, or rather the series of secrets which stem from the forged marriage entry in the register at Old Welmingham Church. His false claim to the title of baronet must not be discovered, Anne Catherick must be put away safely in an asylum, her mother's silence must be bought – the stress of sustaining all these deceits exacerbates the irritability of his nature. His death, trapped in the blazing vestry and consumed by the same flames which consume the secret of his forgery, is melodramatic but undeniably exciting, and it must have been an intriguing possibility in the minds of Victorian readers that the roasting he received on earth might be but a gentle preparation for a more severe roasting to come.

Mr FREDERICK FAIRLIE

(See pp. 65–6 for Walter's fine pen portrait of Mr Fairlie.)
Mr Fairlie has two large collections in his possession: one consists

of valuable art treasures, and the other is a collection of phobias and affectations which are the despair of all those who deal with him. He is inordinately proud and possessive of all of these and they are the pillars of his existence. His art treasures are, by any standard, remarkable. They include paintings by Raphael, English watercolours, furniture and jewellery. He sees himself as the only fit possessor and admirer of them, and the general public are allowed to see only photographs of the originals.

His phobias include a dread of noise ('"Creaking shoes invariably upset me for the day"' (p. 362)), a rare sensitivity to smell (he cannot bear drawings smelling '"of horrid dealers' and brokers' fingers"' (p. 69)) and an equally sensitive reaction to sunlight; hence his existence inside a peculiar cocoon, a thick carpet underneath him and two sets of curtains around him. Ideally Mr Fairlie would like to be insulated from all forms of human contact and emotion – he finds the prospect of tears from Laura (p. 215) or Fanny (p. 362) quite alarming.

His eccentricity certainly adds to the humour of the novel, and provides some relief from Walter's earnestness. Thus his spectacular underestimate of Count Fosco's tenacity on his unexpected arrival at Limmeridge – '"Louis," I said, "do you think he would go away if you gave him five shillings?"' (p. 369) – is delightfully ironic and revealing. This is matched later by his account of Fosco:

> He looked like a walking-West-Indian-epidemic. He was big enough to carry typhus by the ton, and to dye the very carpet he walked on with scarlet fever. In certain emergencies my mind is remarkably soon made up. I instantly determined to get rid of him. (p. 373)

The contribution he makes to the narrative (pp. 360–78) gives him the opportunity to harp on his favourite themes – the delicacy of his nerves, the demands which others are always making upon him and the barbarity of the lower classes and their manners. It expresses his selfish affectation perfectly, and can be juxtaposed against Walter's selflessness instructively. His eccentricity is rarely endearing, unlike Pesca's; his refusal to recognize his niece Laura after her rescue from the asylum is exasperating in the extreme, while the meanness of his wedding gift on her marriage to Sir Percival is really wounding (see Marian's forceful comments, pp. 214–15). Sir Percival's judgements are not always to be trusted, but on this occasion his assessment of Frederick Fairlie is bluntly accurate: '"I'll tell you what he is. He's a maudlin, twaddling, selfish fool, and bores everybody who comes near him about the state of his health"' (p. 348). His death, which enables Laura and Walter to inherit Limmeridge and re-create their earlier happiness, is his only significant contribution to the happiness of others.

LAURA FAIRLIE

Laura is an ideal for Walter: she represents everything which he desires in a woman. She is fair (her name emphasizes the fact), beautiful without being quite perfect, and completely honest and innocent. Walter is captivated by 'the charm of her fair face and head, her sweet expression, and her winning simplicity of manner' (p. 76), and when she declares to him '"I shall believe all that you say to me,"' he has 'the key to her whole character: to that generous trust in others which, in her nature, grew innocently out of the sense of her own truth' (p. 78). From that moment they love each other and recognize that love.

Laura's blameless and innocent character is not her only asset. She is a highly gifted musician, and on the eve of Walter's departure she uses that gift to express the feelings which her words cannot really encompass, and which in any case cannot be made public (p. 145). They have a mutual respect for each other's artistic abilities. On occasion Laura can display courage: as Walter notes as he is about to leave Limmeridge, 'with that courage which women lose so often in the small emergency, and so seldom in the great, she came on nearer to me' (p. 148). Again, in her decision to tell Sir Percival that she can never love him she impresses Marian with her resolution: '"Courage, dear, to tell the truth"' (p. 185). Nor is she without sympathy and understanding for others. On meeting Anne Catherick

(p. 301) her pity for that poor creature is genuine and heartfelt, perhaps because she feels the suffering of her 'double' especially keenly. It is to her credit that she doubts Fosco from the start; her letters to Marian show that she does not fall under the spell of the charismatic Count, as Marian almost does; for, as Marian notes, 'Laura has preserved ... the child's subtle faculty of knowing a friend by instinct, and if I am right in assuming that her first impression of Count Fosco has not been favourable, I for one am in some danger of doubting and distrusting that illustrious foreigner' (pp. 224–5).

Laura gains sympathy in the eyes of the reader as a result of the treatment she receives at the hands of Sir Percival, on honeymoon, at Blackwater Park where she is abused and imprisoned in her own room, and finally, and most cruelly, when she is committed to the asylum in the guise of Anne Catherick. She is Walter's constant inspiration, but most readers now are likely to find her an insipid and uninspiring creation. Her beauty and innocence do not really compensate for the helplessness and frailty which she shows so often. Walter's taking up of the cause of someone unable to help herself throws a heroic light on him, and his almost disinterested concern 'to right an infamous wrong' must be applauded, but his prize may not be the pearl of great price.

PROFESSOR PESCA

Professor Pesca is one of the members of Collins's gallery of eccentrics, a delightful creation, full of energy and good nature. His Italian origins and membership of the Brotherhood are features he has in common with Fosco, but there the similarities end, for the diminutive Pesca is motivated by kindness and a desire to please, where Fosco is never happier than when locked in a battle with an opponent. The professor's name resembles the Italian for fish, and the fact that he is rescued from drowning by Walter may be another joke of the 'Fosco' kind.

The gratitude which Pesca feels towards Walter for having saved his life finds expression in two ways: it is Pesca who enables Walter to obtain the job of drawing master at Limmeridge, and it is Pesca who, albeit reluctantly, reveals the existence of the Brotherhood and Fosco's secret, which gives Walter a perfect bargaining counter in his tussle with the Count. Pesca belongs to an in-between world, of talented servants to the aristocratic and the rich, and their children, a world which Walter also inhabits until his move to Limmeridge. As a foreigner he may not be quite as sensitive as Walter to the nuances of social hierarchy, but he can appreciate the significance of Walter's being treated 'on the footing of a gentleman' at Limmeridge — a circumstance out of the ordinary. His struggle with the English language and with English customs is a pleasure to the reader, and his exuberant performance in front of Walter's mother and sister (pp. 39–42) gives a lively and humorous start to the novel.

Mrs CATHERICK

(See pp. 503–11 for Walter's meeting with Mrs Catherick; and pp. 548–60 for Mrs Catherick's letter to Walter.)

Mrs Catherick is determined to secure outward social respectability at Old Welmingham, and consequently devotes her considerable tenacity and will-power to that end. Her character, however, as it is revealed in her past actions and through her own remarks, is neither admirable nor deserving of public approval. In the past she has had an affair with Philip Fairlie, 'one of the handsomest men in England' (p. 656) and as a result given birth to her daughter Anne, whose illegitimacy is concealed by her marriage to Mr Catherick, a good man whom she considers beneath her. She shows little love for her husband ('I had a contemptible fool for a husband' (p. 559)), or for Anne ('I do not profess to have been at all over-fond of my late daughter' (p. 554)), or even gratitude towards the kind Mrs Clements ('a foolish woman' (p. 505)).

She is used by Sir Percival, whom she finds attractive, to obtain the keys to the vestry; and she allows him to forge the entry in the marriage register, thus becoming his accomplice, as he reminds her.

Although she knows his secret she is unable to take full advantage of the fact. He continues to buy her silence and continued residence at Old Welmingham with an allowance, just as he bought her co-operation in the first place. She becomes the victim of her own greed – note her love of expensive possessions (e.g. p. 560) – and a slave to her own need for society's approbation.

Her interview with Walter and the letter she sends him reveal her singleminded and ruthless pursuit of her ambition, and the declaration '"I mean to make the clergyman's wife bow to me next"' (p. 560) emerges as a fierce threat. Her strength may be less well-disguised than Fosco's but it is scarcely less potent, and among the minor characters in the novel she stands out as a fully realized creation.

ANNE CATHERICK   Importance – two fold.

(See pp. 47–55 for Walter's first encounter with her.)

Anne Catherick, the woman in white, is vital to the plot. By meeting her by accident, and then discovering her identity, Walter learns of Sir Percival's secret. Secondly, her remarkable resemblance to Laura Fairlie is exploited by Count Fosco in order to fake Laura's death. Her '"intellect is not well developed"' (p. 84) but nor is she insane as Sir Percival would like it to be thought. It is her belief in the goodness of Mrs Fairlie (in whose memory she always wears white) and the evil of Sir Percival (whose guilty secret she knows of, but does not understand) which forms the basis of her character. She clings tenaciously to both these beliefs and her convictions reinforce Walter's own. She is touching in her innocence and frailty, and her weakness is used to reveal the true instincts of those who meet her: thus Walter, Laura and Mrs Clements all treat her kindly and with compassion, whereas her own mother and Sir Percival are at best indifferent, and on occasion openly cruel. As Laura's 'twin' she also provides a haunting vision of what might have happened had not Walter and Marian intervened.

Mr GILMORE

(See pp. 150–84 for his contribution to the narrative.)

Mr Gilmore is the Fairlie family solicitor: it is he who reveals the intricacies of the estate, and alerts the reader to the large sums which Sir Percival and Mme Fosco might gain were Laura to die childless. He is a good man whose doubts and misgivings about Sir Percival develop simultaneously with Marian's and the reader's. Walter's description of him follows the pattern of working from a description of external appearance towards an understanding of the inner man – a technique greatly favoured by nineteenth-century novelists (see for example Dickens's portrayal of Captain Cuttle in *Dombey and Son*, Penguin edn, pp 96–7). In Mr Gilmore's case the outward vision may be 'the exact opposite of the conventional idea of an old lawyer' (p. 139), but it gives an accurate idea of his fastidious approach to his job as well as hinting at more sympathetic qualities. His investigations to find out the extent of Sir Percival's debts, and his attempts to prod Mr Fairlie into action, show his fondness for Laura: 'I was determined to spare no personal sacrifice in her service' (p. 177). His reiterated warning to Mr Fairlie – '"... no daughter of mine should be married to any man alive under such a settlement"' (p. 183) – is a heart-rending expression of his powerlessness to prevent the marriage, and it may not be idle speculation to draw a connection between his worries about Laura and his subsequent illness. For the rest of the novel he is convalescing in Germany, and the family's legal affairs are in the hands of Mr Kyrle. He is made godfather to Walter Hartright junior – a fitting reward for his earlier services and loyalty.

Mrs VESEY

Mrs Vesey is Laura's former governess, now a permanent resident at Limmeridge. She is an elderly woman, completely without malice or vitality. She proves an ideal subject for Marian's wit when Walter is introduced to Limmeridge: '"Mrs Vesey is an excellent person, who

possesses all the cardinal virtues and counts for nothing"' (p. 61).
(Note the play on the words 'cardinal' and 'counts'.) Even Walter
is moved to some gently ironic comments: 'Good Mrs Vesey (always
the first of the party to sit down) took possession of an armchair in
a corner, and dozed off comfortably to sleep.' But it is the fact of
his kindness and attention to her (p. 146) which proves his worth;
and when it is revealed that she has been knitting a beautiful Shetland
shawl in secret, as a wedding present for Laura, her own goodness
is made evident (compare Mr Fairlie's wedding gift (p. 214)). After
the wedding Mrs Vesey lives with her unmarried sister at Clapham.
Laura writes to her asking if she can stay there when she is reluctant
to spend a night under the Foscos' roof (p. 407), but she is abducted
before reaching her destination. In a neat touch, Mrs Vesey is present
at the christening of Walter Hartright junior, and reunited with all
the members of the happy house party at Limmeridge (p. 644).

Mr MERRIMAN

(See pp. 175–7 for his visit to Mr Gilmore.)

Mr Merriman is Sir Percival Glyde's solicitor and a lawyer of a
very different kind from Mr Gilmore, through whose discerning gaze
he is presented to the reader. During their encounter, Mr Merriman
adopts 'a manner of inveterate good humour', a ploy similar to the
one used by Sir Percival himself during his courtship of Laura, and
acts as if he bears no responsibility for enforcing his client's instructions (this is another example of Collins's carefully chosen surnames).
Beneath this carefully contrived façade, however, the picture of a
'sharp practitioner' dedicated to the cause of self-enrichment can be
discerned: his reassurances and disclaimers ring hollowly around
the chamber and are in sharp contrast to Mr Gilmore's genuine
feelings of doubt and misgiving. Mr Merriman 'walked to the fire-
place and warmed himself, humming the fag end of a tune in a rich
convivial bass voice' (p. 176), a detail which will be picked up and
expanded by Collins in his portrayal of Count Fosco – in this scene

it lends colour and works in counterpoint to Mr Gilmore's worry and concern.

Mme FOSCO

(See pp. 238–9 for Marian's description of her.)

Mme Fosco, and through her the Count, stand to gain £10,000 from the Fairlie estate, in the event of Laura dying before her, and so she is central to the plot. Before her marriage she had been, according to Marian, 'one of the most impertinent women I ever met with – capricious, exacting and vain to the last degree of absurdity' (p. 212), but the Count has tamed the tiger, for throughout the story she is submissive to his will. She is also an extremely useful ally and servant in carrying out her husband's schemes; she engages Marian in conversation while he reads the letters in the postbag, follows her to the inn where she drugs Fanny and is involved in the substitution of Anne Catherick for Laura in London.

Mme Fosco's character is conveyed to the reader more by her looks and glances, 'her insolent smile' (p. 338) and her actions, 'rolling up endless cigarettes for the Count's own particular smoking' (pp. 239, 252), than through her words, of which there are few. It is her continuing devotion to Count Fosco, even after his death, which testifies to his impact and power.

Mrs RUBELLE

(See pp. 384–5.)

Mrs Rubelle is a sinister figure whose first appearance is in the guise of nurse to Marian Halcombe, an arrangement which has been engineered by Count Fosco. Her character is presented through the filter of Mrs Michelson's conscience-stricken gaze, and the latter can be felt battling against her instincts in her description of Mrs Rubelle

on pp. 384–5 and, as it proves, against her better judgement. Fosco
reveals in his confession how he used Mrs Rubelle to move Marian
in the middle of the night into an unoccupied part of Blackwater Park,
and later how the Rubelles' London house was used in the plot to
substitute Laura for Anne Catherick. Her husband is Fosco's agent
and is used to retrieve the incriminating letter from Pesca (pp. 616–17).
As a couple they provide Fosco with invaluable support, and they
are figures from that shadowy, continental background from which
he emerges so colourfully.

Mrs MICHELSON

(See pp. 379–420 for her narrative.)

As housekeeper at Blackwater Park during Marian's illness, Mrs
Michelson advances the story to the moment when Laura is sent to
London under the illusion that Marian will be there to meet her.
During this time Mrs Michelson is conveniently removed from Blackwater under the pretext of finding cheap lodgings suitable for
convalescence in Torquay, so that the Count can contrive Laura's
departure to London. She confirms the impression of Sir Percival as
a violent and unpredictable man, while her opinion of the Count is
highly favourable. It is clear that this pious clergyman's widow has
fallen under Fosco's spell: according to her he has 'a truly Christian
meekness of temper' (p. 380) and 'the manners of a true nobleman'
(p. 381). Her husband's sermons, which form the basis of her response
to most events, are obviously not proof against the charms of Fosco.
Fosco writes:

> Mrs Michelson believed in me from first to last. This ladylike person (widow
> of a Protestant priest), overflowed with faith. Touched by such superfluity
> of simple confidence in a woman of her mature years, I opened the ample
> reservoirs of my nature and absorbed it all. (p. 621)

With just a few details, like the texts of her husband's sermons ('Judge
not that ye be not judged'; 'Do as you would be done by') Collins

can create the picture of a whole life and marriage; and within a few pages he has established in Mrs Michelson a credible and convincing character.

Mrs CLEMENTS

(See pp. 123–4, 129–30. For her account of what finally happened to Anne Catherick, see pp. 479–85; for her story of Mrs Catherick see pp. 485–98.)

Mrs Clements is Anne Catherick's surrogate mother. She acts as Anne's protector and friend throughout, and her distress at Anne's death is in marked contrast to Mrs Catherick's callous unconcern (p. 505). There is hardly any physical description of Mrs Clements: her character emerges through her words, her expressions and, of course, her actions. At Walter's first meeting with her she gives him a firm reprimand for frightening Anne – an indication of her love for that disturbed girl and the directness which does her credit. She does not reappear until the Third Epoch (pp. 479–98), when she is interviewed by Walter, who is trying to establish the sequence of events at Blackwater Park leading up to Laura's disappearance. Her account of Anne's abduction by Fosco is almost entirely in the form of reported speech, which means that very little new is learnt about her character, though it serves a useful purpose in reminding the reader of key events. The following chapter, however, does contain her own words; they are genuine, heartfelt and, when she is told of Anne's death, moving: '"I made her first short frocks. I taught her to walk. The first time she ever said Mother it was to *me*"' (p. 497). Such reminiscences make the impact of her emotion almost unbearable. Unfortunately her simplicity also makes her an easy subject for Fosco to manipulate. Collins gives a picture of simple goodness, but he knows that simple goodness has its limitations.

THE VESTRY CLERK

(See pp. 516–23.)

Although he is not given a name, the vestry clerk who shows Walter the Old Welmingham register and informs him of the duplicate in Knowlesbury is a vivid and colourful creation. 'He was a cheerful, familiar, loudly talkative old man, with a very poor opinion (as I soon discovered) of the place in which he lived, and a happy sense of superiority to his neighbours in virtue of the great personal distinction of having once been in London' (p. 516). He has a good knowledge of local affairs and a keen desire to catch up on the news from London, as he has been away for some '"five and twenty years"'. Walter is anxious to see the register and not to embark on a long conversation. The contrast between the clerk's languid and easygoing approach to his life and Walter's intense and agitated pursuit of Sir Percival increases the tension of the scene. It is a further example of Walter's abundant kindness that he remembers to slip 'a little present' into his hand on leaving.

Collins uses the clerk again during the fire scene, where his paralysis and sense of doom is in sharp contrast to Walter's efforts to save Sir Percival. He acts, along with the other villagers, as a chorus of doom and despair against which Walter vainly struggles.

Commentary

Form

The Woman in White is a highly organized and beautifully constructed novel. It is true that some critics and readers have found the complex mechanics of its plots over-dominant. Anthony Trollope wrote:

... but I can never lose the taste of the construction. The author seems always warning me to remember that something happened at exactly half past two o'clock on Tuesday morning, or that a woman disappeared from the road just fifteen yards beyond the fourth milestone. (*Autobiography*, ii, 82)

This is a judgement which would have upset Collins as his declared purpose was to create a novel in which the telling of a complicated story and the delineation of character were equally important. Quite as many critics, though, have admired its considerable merits.

In this context, the use of a multiple narrative scheme is worth examining in some detail. The device is neither original nor peculiar to Collins (Dickens, for example, employed two narrators in *Bleak House* (1853), one writing in the present tense, the other, a character called Esther Summerson, writing in the past tense) – but it is integral to the work. It enables Collins to present the story in the way he wishes and 'to trace the course of one complete series of events by making the persons who have been most closely connected with them, at each successive stage, relate their own experience, word for word' (p. 33). It also enables him to include a wide variety of literary modes: diaries (such as Walter's and Marian's) form the largest group; but there are also letters; the recorded statement of an illiterate cook; the words from a tombstone; statements obtained after the event by Walter from such diverse characters and stylists as Mr Gilmore, Mr Fairlie, Mrs Catherick and Count Fosco. All of these are embedded in the novel, lending substance and authenticity to the events. Authenticity is a quality highly prized by Collins, despite his reputation for the sensational and the melodramatic, and it is in *The Woman in White* and *The Moonstone* that he comes closest to that goal.

The narration belongs chiefly to the 'good' characters, as befits a novel in which good eventually triumphs over evil, and the good characters survive to enjoy a happy ending while the bad die. The bulk of the narrative is shared by Walter and Marian, and their steadfast loyalty to Laura, to each other and to Christian values helps to form the reader's opinion of characters and events. All the contributors reveal themselves through their narratives: Walter's is straightforward and candid; the man is the style. Likewise, Marian's diary is exactly the appropriate medium for the first entrance of Count Fosco into the story: his unique attributes need to be seen and recorded by a sensitive and talented writer, as he himself is the first to acknowledge! The real benefits of the scheme are more evident when characters like Mr Fairlie make their contribution (pp. 360–78). The reader is given, like a listener in an opera house, a chance to hear a different voice – one that is an integral part of the story, necessary to the action, related to the development of the plot, but in another key, with an altered emphasis and rhythm. In this particular case, the reader can enjoy a glimpse of the world as seen through Mr Fairlie's eyes and be amused by the distorting effect which follows. Just as the fairground mirror gives a recognizable but out-of-proportion view of ourselves, so Mr Fairlie's view of events and people is out of proportion to their real significance, but none the less revealing. Shakespeare is the master of scene-patterning (the placing of one scene to reflect another, or the juxtaposition of comic and tragic), and Collins shows himself able to use the same sort of technique in the novel. Consider, for example, the narrative contributions made by Mrs Catherick, and, in particular, Count Fosco. Fosco's arrogant account (the astonishing list of titles which precede his narrative (p. 618) is like the proliferation of medals on the uniform of a South American dictator) laced with whimsicality (the concern for his menagerie) provides some release from the tension of the final confrontation, and gives an imaginative dimension to the novel which is beyond Walter's essentially earth-bound style. The overall result of this device of multiple narration is that both characters and events are often seen from more than one perspective, adding to their depth and increasing our understanding and appreciation.

The story is continuous with each section dovetailing neatly into the next, but the narrative scheme does allow for events to be reviewed and for key points to be revealed or, indeed, repeated from another point of view. Mr Gilmore, for example, gives this version of Walter Hartright's last evening at Limmeridge at the beginning of his narrative:

> I did not see Miss Fairlie until later in the day, at dinner time. She was not looking well, and I was sorry to observe it ... Miss Fairlie played to us in the evening – not so well as usual, I thought. We had a rubber at whist, a mere profanation, so far as play was concerned, of that noble game. I had been favourably impressed by Mr Hartright on our first introduction to one another, but I soon discovered that he was not free from the social failings incidental to his age. There are three things that none of the young men of the present generation can do. They can't sit over their wine, they can't play at whist, and they can't pay a lady a compliment. Mr Hartright was no exception to the general rule. (p. 151)

The reader, of course, is in possession of many more facts than Mr Gilmore and is able to appreciate the causes behind the social failings observed by the recently arrived solicitor. Collins's skill lies in his ability to let Mr Gilmore reveal his own character and disposition, while simultaneously reminding the reader of the main events of that important evening.

The action is continuous throughout the novel but it is the First and Second Epochs which cover most of the ground. In these, all the major characters and locations are introduced and, by the end of the Second Epoch, Count Fosco's plot on behalf of Sir Percival is brought to its apparently successful conclusion. The Third Epoch works differently, and in two ways: it advances the story to the moment Mr and Mrs Walter Hartright and son take possession of Limmeridge; but it also unravels, thanks to Walter's investigation and pursuit of clues, all the various and connecting threads of Sir Percival's history and Count Fosco's plot. It is not until Fosco's narrative appears that the whole pattern can be understood and the reader's curiosity satisfied; and, even then, the mystery of the Brotherhood's revenge is postponed. In adopting this structure, Collins can be seen to be working like a magician, demonstrating a trick in the first two Epochs, and then explaining the mechanics of that trick in all its detail to the further delight of his audience in the third.

Melodrama

The conventions of melodrama would have been familiar to Collins's readership through the popular theatre of the day. The Drury Lane and Covent Garden Theatres covered their costs by putting on panto-mimes, variety shows and melodramas. Throughout the country, plays with titles like *Plot and Passion*, *Lady Audley's Secret* and *The Castle Spectre* were being churned out to delight and amuse a public keen to escape the grind of industrial labour. The plots were absurd, the characters two-dimensional, the setbacks suffered by the hero un-believable, but those were the features, with the all-important happy ending, which the public demanded and which it received in abundance. James L. Smith, in his excellent study of melodrama, gives this formula for a successful melodrama in the theatre:

> Take an innocent man and a defenceless woman, both of them wholly admirable and free from fault. Present them sympathetically so that an audience will identify with them and share their hopes. And then set against them every obstacle you can devise. Persecute them with villains, dog them with ill-luck, thrust them into a hostile world which threatens at every moment their instant annihilation. Dramatize these excitements as effectively as the resources of the stage will allow, heighten the suspense with music, relieve it with laughter and tears. And then when all seems lost, allow your hero and heroine to win. Let villains be outwitted, ill-luck reversed, physical danger overcome and virtue finally rewarded with infinite joy. Present your play honestly, without condescension, and its warm and simple message will help every spectator to face life more courageously than before. (James L. Smith, *Melodrama*, in The Critical Idiom series, Methuen, 1973; p. 15)

Collins's debt to the form is quite clear but in pointing out the features of similarity to that fundamental formula it would be unjust not to acknowledge those areas in which he went beyond it, thereby enhancing the original. Laura and Walter come very close to the pattern of 'an innocent man and a defenceless woman', but, certainly in Walter's case, he achieves a flesh-and-blood reality through Collins's careful and detailed characterization, which was never part of the brief for the authors of dramatic melodramas. Readers will 'identify with them and share their hopes' but Marian is also involved in their sympathies, and she is a creation whose unusual mixture of elements would not have fitted into the black and white vision of stage melodrama. Likewise, Count Fosco, with his hypnotic charm, his compelling conversation, his colour and panache, is far too likeable to be classed alongside Black Ralph from *The Dream at Sea*. Sir Percival Glyde conforms to the stereotype it is true, but there is enough richness elsewhere in the novel (Pesca, Mr Fairlie) for that to be forgotten.

Besides giving most of his characters an imaginative dimension beyond the scope of the melodrama dramatists, Collins's plot-making was more ingenious and coherent than any found on stage (except, of course, dramatization of his own novels!). Identical twins and fantastic coincidences were the staple of melodrama, but Collins works more subtly and teasingly with his readers than the dramatists dared to do with their often ill-educated audiences. The substitution of Anne for Laura is only fully explained at the very end of the book, the details of the plot have remained a mystery, whereas, on stage, all the villain's atrocities would have to have been visible, and 'hissable', too! Naturally, Collins gives his readers a happy ending, fulfilling the hope which has been present from Walter's first meeting with Laura; but the birth of their son and the fact that Walter now possesses Limmeridge's art treasures, not to mention Marian's benign presence, lend more authority to that hackneyed formula than usual.

If Collins had wanted to imitate the form slavishly in *The Woman in White*, he might have dwelt longer on Walter's escapes chronicled so briefly by him at the end of the Second Epoch:

> The vessel was wrecked in the Gulf of Mexico – I was among the few saved from the sea. It was my third escape from peril of death. Death by disease, death by the Indians, death by drowning – all three had approached me; all three had passed me by. (p. 426)

Such adventures would have been perfect material for the ambitious stage-designers of the day and highly popular with an audience which had seen 'Vesuvius in eruption, with lava rushing down the mountain-side into the sea' in *Masaniello* (see Smith, *Melodrama*, pp. 27–31, for a description of some of the more fantastic stage re-creations). But his concessions in this direction only reach as far as Count Fosco's menagerie, a feature contributing more to his humanity than villainy. In the same way, Marian's dream, which foretells Walter's dangers and survivals, has many analogues but is hardly exploited by Collins for maximum effect.

The comic element in melodrama was often unrelated to the main plot: it was an occasion for a funny turn or speciality act to be per-formed, releasing tension, or enabling the scenery to be changed behind the backcloth. Mr Fairlie, Professor Pesca and the vestry clerk all belong to the plot of *The Woman in White* as well as contributing humour to it. *The Woman in White* remains a melodrama, despite all its refinements, but it is because of those refinements that it has survived while the vast bulk of Victorian melodrama gathers dust.

The organization of The Woman in White

The Woman in White can be seen in terms of a battle between 'good' and 'evil' and, in many ways, it resembles a medieval romance, with Walter as the Christian knight, champion of truth, Laura the beautiful and innocent maiden at the mercy of a jealous and angry husband, and Fosco the awesome enemy, possessing almost supernatural powers. All the major characters are involved in a contest where the advantage lies with evil until the final breathtaking confrontation, when good triumphs by a hair's breadth; but its structure is considerably more complex than a simple romance.

The 'double ration' in the novel has often been remarked upon: there are two heroines – Laura and Marian; two villains – Sir Percival and Count Fosco; two vital locations – Limmeridge House and Blackwater Park. This pairing gives Collins the scope to explore and expand his vision. Laura, for instance, is the embodiment of passive goodness; her half-sister, Marian, personifies a much more active and forthright version of the same quality. By rescuing both of them, Walter's achievement becomes all the more praiseworthy, for, without Marian's intelligence and bite, Laura's insipid frailty would be hard to endure.

Examples of this pairing and patterning abound in the novel: the two solicitors, Mr Gilmore and Mr Merriman, one belonging to each camp, may share some legal habits of mind but they are at opposite poles in terms of human sympathy and understanding: Count Fosco and Mr Fairlie are both highly cultured and highly eccentric, but the one is flamboyant and extravagant, the other withdrawn and punctilious. Count Fosco and Professor Pesca are both members of the Brotherhood, and Italian by birth, but the one is Walter's deadly enemy and the other his most ardent friend; Mrs Catherick is Anne's real mother, but she has no affection for her own daughter and abandons her, while Mrs Clements is Anne's surrogate mother and gives all the love she can to the poor, distressed girl. All these echoing and reflecting associations contribute to the thematic richness and density of the novel, and add to the reader's pleasure and appreciation of Collins's art. The most important pattern of relationship, however, is the one between Anne Catherick and Laura Fairlie: their remarkable resemblance to each other, observed at first by Mrs Fairlie, then by Walter and Marian, is the key to Fosco's plot and to the novel. Collins ensures that Laura is made aware of the resemblance:

'While I was looking at her, while she was very close to me, it came over my mind suddenly that we were like each other! Her face was pale and thin and weary – but the sight of it startled me, as if it had been the sight of my own face in the glass after a long illness.' (p. 300)

By bringing them face to face, Collins exploits the coincidence of their similarity and adds a note of pathos as Laura realizes that her sickly double is doomed to die soon.

The same careful organization can be seen in the way Walter's rescue of Professor Pesca is matched by Fosco's rescue of Sir Percival; in the long run the former action actually contributes indirectly to Fosco's exposure and downfall. Even the beautiful summerhouse at Limmeridge, the scene of Walter's first meeting with Laura and the subject of the treasured sketch, has its contrasting counterpart in the rotten boathouse at Blackwater, where the wounded spaniel leaves traces of its blood, Sir Percival discovers Anne's note and Count Fosco deceives kind but simple Mrs Clements. The skill which Collins demonstrates in relating characters, events and locations to each other and to the novel's wider concerns matches his skill in devising the novel's narrative scheme: when both are examined in detail, they confirm his reputation as a master–craftsman.

Limmeridge House and Blackwater Park

Limmeridge House and Blackwater Park are the two pivotal locations in the novel and, just as the characters arrange themselves neatly into 'good' and 'evil', so each house belongs to one of the categories. Like the names of many of the characters, the names of the houses are suggestive of their respective qualities. Blackwater House has obviously evil connotations: it might feature as the home of almost any villain from melodrama. Collins reinforces the impact of its name by including a detailed description of the house and grounds as seen by Marian (pp. 225–8) – a keen and perceptive judge, whose sensibilities have been refined by the time she has spent at beautiful Limmeridge. Various parts of the house are covered in 'dust and dirt'; one wing, which may be architecturally magnificent, is full of 'damp, darkness, and rats'; and, although some of the apartments have been decorated 'in the bright and modern way', the house is 'stifled' by trees – 'They are, for the most part, young, and planted far too thickly.' In other words, the house lacks the joy of sunlight and is condemned to stay in the shade, an emblem of its moral status. Even the flower garden, of which Marian has entertained high hopes, proves to be 'small and poor and ill-kept'. The large, circular fish pond outside the house has a 'leaden monster' in the middle, an image which could be interpreted as representing Sir Percival. Once in the grounds, Marian sees the 'stagnant' waters of the lake itself and the rest of her passage is packed with a series of unpleasant adjectives, 'black ... damp and marshy ... rank ... dismal ... black and poisonous ... rotten ... sickly ... dreary ... shabby'. The total picture is one of unrelieved gloom which matches the 'hideous family portraits' lining the long galleries of the house. Collins clinches his portrait of Black-water Park with the incident of the wounded spaniel: Marian hears the dying animal in the boathouse and, with the help of the house-keeper, tries to save the forlorn creature, but to no avail. 'The misery of a weak, helpless, dumb creature is surely one of the saddest of all the mournful sights which this world can show' (p. 229). Her opinion of the place will always be coloured by the incident, and like the spots of blood which linger on the ground and are noticed by Fosco, the associations will linger in her mind and the reader's. These associations with suffering and death are picked up by Fosco in his powerful speech about undetected crime (pp. 255–6); and it is at Blackwater Park that the Count's plan to trap Laura is formulated. As Marian writes on her first evening at the Park, 'Judging by my vague impressions of the place thus far, it is the exact opposite of Limmeridge' (p. 220).

Limmeridge is the home of the Fairlie family, and its name is light and delicate, like Laura herself. When Walter wakes after his first night in Cumberland and 'drew up my blind, the sea opened before me joyously under the broad August sunlight, and the distant coast of Scotland fringed the horizon with its lines of melting blue' (p. 57). The artist in him responds to the beauty of his surroundings, a beauty which is complemented by his delight in Laura's own beauty. Unlike the dark and dismal galleries of Blackwater, Limmeridge has 'many windows' in its rooms, and glass doors which can be thrown open on to the terrace, where Laura walks during their first happy evening together (p. 85). Outside, there are lawns and the terrace is 'beautifully ornamented along its whole length with a profusion of flowers' (p. 81); even the perimeter of the grounds is marked by 'High, white walls' (p. 429) – such a contrast to the trees of Blackwater Park. The summer-house, built like a miniature Swiss chalet, is the scene of Walter's first view of Laura; it is also where Marian tells Walter of Sir Percival. Walter treasures Laura's sketch of it throughout his exile and he uses it to aid her recovery. Its function as a special place, hallowed by their love, places it as the exact opposite of the boathouse at Black-water, which gathers so many unhappy and unpleasant associations through the course of the plot.

Set out like this, the contrasts may seem to be over-schematic, so carefully matched that a rather boring draw is the only possible result, but it must be remembered that the pictures of the two houses are built up cumulatively throughout the novel and are not delivered complete in every detail. Collins's methods may lack some of the subtleties of Dickens when matching man and mansion, but they are effective within the scope of his novel.

Money and wealth in The Woman in White

Both Sir Percival Glyde and Count Fosco are financially embarrassed at the beginning of the novel, and it is their scheme to secure themselves financially, and the discovery of that scheme by Walter and Marian, which form the main thrust of the story. In Fosco's words,

> The bond of friendship which united Percival and myself was strengthened, on this occasion, by a touching similarity in the pecuniary position on his side and on mine. We both wanted money. Immense necessity! Universal want! (p. 619)

Their attitude towards money, and the lengths they are prepared to go in order to obtain it, reveal their true natures: they are ruthless and prepared to sacrifice human values for material ones.

In complete contrast, Walter, the champion of 'good', dissociates himself from them by declaring 'bluntly': '"There shall be no money motive," I said, "no idea of personal advantage in the service I mean to render to Lady Glyde"' (p. 465). His altruism is eventually rewarded by his inheritance of Limmeridge House but for the early part of the Third Epoch he has to live in poverty and obscurity: the hardships which he endured on his travels are not yet finished. Collins builds up his picture of Walter's, Marian's and Laura's impoverished lifestyle at this point in the novel through his use of adjectives, much as he does in Marian's description of Blackwater: 'poor', 'small', 'humblest', 'cheap' chime through the early chapters of this section. Marian, too, must undergo hardships: she takes on the housework:

> 'What a woman's hands *are* fit for,' she said, 'early and late these hands of mine shall do.' They trembled as she held them out. The wasted arms told their sad story of the past, as she turned up the sleeves of the poor, plain dress that she wore for safety's sake; but the unquenchable spirit of the woman burnt bright in her even yet. (p. 453)

Walter and Marian are united by their love for Laura and regard for each other. In practical terms, they pool their savings, as a fund which will finance their effort 'to right an infamous wrong'. 'We calculated our weekly expenditure to the last farthing, and we never touched our little fund except in Laura's interests and for Laura's sake' (p. 453). Their use of money is for the benefit of another and is the complete opposite of the self-interest which motivates Sir Percival and Count Fosco. Walter is even prepared to use some of his earnings to buy some of Laura's sketches:

I set aside a little weekly tribute from my earnings, to be offered to her as the price paid by strangers for the poor, faint, valueless sketches, of which I was the only purchaser ... I have all those hidden drawings in my possession still – they are my treasures beyond price. (pp. 499–500)

Marian's determination to rescue Laura from the asylum forces her to bribe the nurse. The sum involved is £400, more than half of Marian's total wealth, and the sum enables the nurse to start in business with her fiancé immediately. Such selfless behaviour is difficult to detect in either Frederick Fairlie or Mrs Catherick.

Frederick Fairlie has wealth and money, which he enjoys in almost complete solitude. His is a self-centred, virtually solipsistic existence, and his chief delight is his ownership of his collection of art treasures. Despite providing a great deal of the novel's humour, it is necessary to the scheme of the novel that he should die and his wealth be passed on to more deserving people. His art treasures will ultimately belong to an artist who will understand and appreciate them fully, namely, Walter; and Limmeridge House, and its grounds, will again be a home for children, and a fitting reward for the sufferings endured by Laura and Marian.

Mrs Catherick's life is orientated towards money and respectability: as she herself admits, 'I liked my presents and I wanted more' (p. 549). This passion for Sir Percival's gifts and, in particular, her longing for a gold watch, contribute to her becoming his accomplice and condemn her to a life at Old Welmingham dedicated to retrieving her reputation. She is able to pride herself that she 'had a better income, a better house over my head, better carpets on my floors, than half the women who turned up the whites of their eyes at the sight of me. The dress of virtue, in our parts, was cotton print. I had silk' (p. 554) – thanks to Sir Percival's handsome allowance. The reader's impression is of a soulless and frighteningly singleminded life: she may have achieved respectability, but at the cost of her humanity.

The 'good' characters are those who use money not as an end, but as a means towards a higher goal – in the case of Walter and Laura, this is the triumph of love over adversity. During the fire at the vestry, Walter is even prepared to offer a financial incentive to the villagers, paralysed by the sight of the fire and Sir Percival's screams: '"Five shillings apiece to every man who helps me ..." They started into life at the words' (p. 537). Revenge is never part of Walter's make-up, even when the victim, Sir Percival, deserves the retribution which he is suffering. The 'evil' characters are those who subordinate everything to their love of wealth and money. It is because Count Fosco has so many other motivations that it is difficult to place him in that simple category.

Art and artists in The Woman in White

The 'good' characters share something else besides their indifference to material wealth. Walter, Marian and Laura are all artists in some way. Walter earns his living as a drawing master, as did his father (and, indeed, Collins's own father), and it is his skill which brings him to Limmeridge and Laura. His sensibility makes his appreciation of Laura and her beauty stronger and better informed, while, at the same time, he is aware of the inadequacy of his own sketch of her. As the new master of Limmeridge, its art treasures will be in the hands of a practical connoisseur, one quite removed from the dilettante excesses of Mr Fairlie.

Laura's sketches may be 'poor', 'faint', and 'valueless', but she is an accomplished musician. It is while she is playing 'the heavenly tenderness of the music of Mozart' (p. 81) that Walter's feelings are transported: 'It was an evening of sights and sounds never to forget' (p. 81). When Walter has to leave Limmeridge before Sir Percival's arrival, Laura insists on playing for him again: '"Don't speak of tomorrow," she said. "Let the music speak to us tonight in a happier

language than ours"' (p. 145). She falters while playing but is determined to continue: she cannot communicate her feelings of love,
frustration and loss in any other way – the presence of Mr Gilmore,
convention and her own shyness prevent her. Walter continues:

> Sometimes her fingers touched the notes with a lingering fondness – a
> soft, plaintive, dying tenderness, unutterably beautiful and mournful to hear:
> sometimes they faltered and failed her, or hurried over the instrument
> mechanically, as if their task was a burden to them. (p. 146)

He is not deaf to the music or the message which Laura is conveying
to him through it. Her playing has another admirer, Count Fosco:

> He sat by the piano, with his watch-chain resting in folds, like a golden
> serpent, on the sea-green protuberance of his waistcoat. His immense head
> lay languidly on one side, and he gently beat time with two of his yellow-white
> fingers. He highly approved of the music, and tenderly admired Laura's
> manner of playing. (p. 309)

Marian's artistic skill is to be found in her writing and, in case the
reader is not fully aware of her talents, her admirer Count Fosco's
postscript to her diary leaves no doubts. He notes 'the wonderful
power of memory, the accurate observation of character, the easy
grace of style, the charming outbursts of womanly feeling ... The
presentation of my own character is masterly in the extreme'
(pp. 358–9). As we have already noted, Marian tells more of the story
than any other narrator except Walter, and her style, which is slightly
more emotional and vivid than his, is a fine example of the way
Collins develops his characters through their own words. (Examine
her portrait of Fosco and the way her fascination with him becomes
the reader's own (pp. 239–43).)

Significantly, of all the 'evil' characters, it is Fosco who is most
like an artist. He often sings snatches from opera, he plays the piano,
writes engagingly – if idiosyncratically – and is not afraid to give his
opinion on any cultural topic. Marian's description of the Count's
performance at the piano is revealing:

> ... he began thundering on the piano, and singing to it with loud and
> lofty enthusiasm – only interrupting himself, at intervals, to announce to me

fiercely the titles of the different pieces of music ... The piano trembled under his powerful hands, and the tea cups on the table rattled, as his big bass voice thundered out the notes, and his heavy foot beat time on the floor. (p. 336)

The features which emerge from this delicately satirical passage are not the music itself, but the other sounds to which the Count seems oblivious, but which Marian cannot help registering. His visit to the opera, critical in the chain of events leading to his assassination, is an occasion which he uses to flatter his vanity – his delight in music is not like Walter's simple, heartfelt appreciation: 'He looked about him, at the pauses in the music, serenely satisfied with himself and his fellow creatures' (p. 590). (The whole of this scene is an example of Collins at his best and Fosco at his most memorable; it repays several readings.)

The end of the novel sees the concentration of all three artists at Limmeridge, itself a place of beauty; and it is clear that Walter Hartright junior will not have a culturally deprived background.

Chance, coincidence and accident

All melodramas rely on elements of chance as a basis for their plots and *The Woman in White* is no exception. The most obvious example of the influence which chance wields over an individual and his destiny is Walter's first encounter with Anne Catherick at the Hampstead crossroads. Were it not such 'a close and sultry night', Walter would have taken the shortest route home, avoiding the heath and so missing the strange woman whose life was to become so closely involved with his own. As the plot develops, both Walter and the reader share the feeling that he is part of a larger drama – at one stage its victim, ultimately its hero, but never fully in control of its direction; only the author (or perhaps his alter ego, Fosco) is able to do that. Note Fosco's remarks at the beginning of his confession, 'What are we (I ask) but puppets in a show-box? Oh, omnipotent Destiny, pull our strings gently! Dance us mercifully off our miserable little stage! The preceding lines, rightly understood, express an entire system of philosophy. It is mine' (p. 619).

Coincidence is central to the plot in two ways. The uncanny

resemblance between Laura Fairlie and Anne Catherick is exploited by Count Fosco to effect his substitution and gain the huge sums of money which he and Sir Percival desire. This coincidence is developed further when it is revealed that they had the same father, the handsome Philip Fairlie. The second crucial coincidence involves the reunion of Walter, Marian and Laura at Limmeridge churchyard in front of 'Laura's' tombstone. Without this chance meeting, it might have been several months before Walter had traced Marian, time for Sir Percival and the Count to make themselves completely safe. Obviously, the symbolic significance of their meeting at Limmeridge and in front of Laura's own grave is important in the novel, but the use of coincidence also suggests that all three of them have an almost telepathic communication with each other, drawing them simultaneously to the same place.

There are two accidents described in the novel which have a crucial bearing on the plot. The first is Pesca's near-drowning at Brighton: 'We had met there accidentally and were bathing together' (p. 36). In his enthusiasm to copy the English in all their amusements, Pesca attempts to swim, nearly drowns and is saved by Walter's prompt action. As a result, Pesca feels a deep sense of gratitude to his friend and repays it firstly by recommending him for the job at Limmeridge, and secondly by later revealing the existence of the Brotherhood, which enables Walter to extract a 'confession' from Fosco. These events are mirrored in the relationship between Count Fosco and Sir Percival Glyde. Fosco's 'accidental presence, years ago, on the steps of the Trinità del Monte at Rome, assisted Sir Percival's escape from robbery and assassination at the critical moment when he was wounded in the hand, and might the next instant have been wounded in the heart' (p. 213). As a result of this, Sir Percival feels a sense of gratitude towards Fosco which leads to the plot which they formulate together. Significantly, it is Walter's saving of a good man which ultimately leads to Fosco's exposure – good finally defeats evil, as the convention of melodrama demanded.

The macabre in The Woman in White

Chapter XII of the First Epoch (pp. 116–30) is well worth studying in detail for its extraordinary accumulation of macabre and lurid details. It culminates with Anne Catherick kissing and cleaning Mrs Fairlie's gravestone: 'Under the wan wild evening light, that woman and I were met together again, a grave between us, the dead about us, the lonesome hills closing us round on every side' (p. 119). Collins was undoubtedly satisfying a popular taste by including such scenes – stage melodramas and Gothic novels had created an audience for gruesome exhibitions, and the same audience enjoyed the genius of Edgar Allan Poe, in stories like 'The Fall of the House of Usher' and 'The Murders in the Rue Morgue'.

The inclusion of this scene in *The Woman in White* was not simply a device to attract a larger readership. The reunion of Walter, Laura and Marian in that same Limmeridge churchyard beside Laura's grave (pp. 430–31) reminds the attentive reader of the earlier occasion, so that joy is tinged by the sad certainty that Anne is dead; furthermore, Laura, in her sickness, now resembles her more closely than ever. The churchyard resonates with memories and associations, another indication of Collins's evocative use of place. The same economical power can be seen in the penultimate chapter of the novel (pp. 640–44) describing Fosco's violent death and his lying, almost in state, in the Paris morgue. Stripped of his clothes, his title and of life, Fosco still dominates the scene. Walter reports, 'For a few moments, but not for longer, I forced myself to see these things through the glass screen' (p. 643).

Pathetic fallacy

This is a common term in literary criticism and, although it was first coined in 1856, it is a device which had been in use much earlier. The term was invented by the influential artist and critic John Ruskin, in his work *Modern Painters*: 'All violent feelings produce . . . a falseness in . . . impressions of external things which I would generally characterize as the Pathetic Fallacy.' Put more simply, if less elegantly, people's mood or state of mind influences their perception of landscape and surroundings. Collins uses this device, most notably on the eve of Walter's departure from Limmeridge, when Walter retraces the steps of his outings with Laura:

I went on to the avenue of trees, where we had breathed together the warm
fragrance of August evenings, where we had admired together the myriad
combinations of shade and sunlight that dappled the ground at our feet. The
leaves fell about me from the groaning branches, and the earthy decay in the
atmosphere chilled me to the bones ... I gained the summit of the hill, and
looked at the view which we had so often admired in the happier time. It
was cold and barren – it was no longer the view I remembered. The sunshine
of her presence was far from me – the charm of her voice no longer murmured
in my ear ... Was the view that I had seen, while listening to those words,
the view that I saw now, standing on the hilltop by myself? ... Wind and
wave had long since smoothed out the trace of her which she had left in
those marks on the sand. I looked over the wide monotony of the seaside
prospect, and the place in which we two had idled away the sunny hours
was as lost to me as if I had never known it, as strange to me as if I stood
already on a foreign shore. (pp. 140–41)

As an artist, Walter is particularly sensitive to his surroundings
and to his perception of them, and his sense of desolation and disappointment is made all the more poignant on his solitary walk
over ground which had such happy associations in the past. In
Shakespeare's plays, violent weather in the heavens usually signifies
upheavals on earth (e.g. in *King Lear*, *The Tempest*, *Julius Caesar*).
Collins uses a similar idea when, for example, Mr Gilmore returns to
Limmeridge in a final attempt to persuade Mr Fairlie to change his
mind: 'The wind howled dismally all night, and strange cracking and
groaning noises sounded here, there, and everywhere in the empty
house' (p. 179). The interview with Mr Fairlie is doomed and the
state of the weather underlines the reader's fears that nothing can
prevent Sir Percival from marrying Laura immediately.

The vivid sense of place, felt by all the characters, adds greatly to
the melodramatic atmosphere of the whole novel.

Glossary

Alexander the Great (356–323 B.C.)
King of Macedonia; great military
leader

Allegorical leaden monster: statue
of a character from mythology

Aneurism: swelling (in this case of
the heart)

Ante-chamber: room before or
leading to the main apartment

Apologist: defender, counsel or
spokesman

Arl: all

Asseveration: solemn declaration

Asylum: place of safety, refuge
(it has come to be synonymous
with an institution for the
insane). A private asylum is an
institution run for profit, not
necessarily by a well-qualified
person

Barber of Seville: opera by Rossini
(1792–1868)

Benjamin: youngest in a family,
often the favourite

Boudoir: a small, elegantly furnished
room, where a lady might retire
to be alone, or to receive her
intimate friends

Brougham: a one-horse closed
carriage

Cambric: fine white linen

Caprice: whim; sudden change of
mind for no good reason

Card case: small case containing a
visiting card

Cardinal virtues: justice, temperance,
fortitude, patience

Carpet bag: a travelling bag or
case made from carpet pieces

Cast my insular skin: no longer
English in my taste

Chattels: movable property or
possessions

Chatterton: (1752–70) English poet
who committed suicide at the
age of seventeen

Chi sa? who knows?

Chiffonier: A small cupboard or
sideboard

Clandestine: secret

Clap traps: literally, a trick to
obtain applause in the
theatre

Crape: black silk for mourning

Credential: letter of introduction

Creole: of mixed European and
West Indian blood

Crochets: probably a misprint for
crotchets, a peculiar personal
whim or opinion

Daniel iv: 18–25: Daniel's interpretation of King Nebuchadnezzar's dream about a tree growing into heaven

Dead Sea: landlocked sea, with no outlets and no fish – below sea level and extremely salty

Depository: guardian, trustee

Dog cart: an open cart for ordinary driving, with two back to back seats across its width

Donizetti: Italian composer of Opera (1797–1848)

Dorcas Society: a ladies' association in church for the purpose of making and providing clothes for the poor: only the completely respectable could be members

Dresden china: a variety of white porcelain, made at Meissen near Dresden, and characterized by elaborate decoration and figure pieces in delicate colouring, like Mr Fairlie himself!

East India man: ship of large tonnage trading between England and the East Indies

Écarté: card game for two players

Eulogy: praise

Exhibition of 1851: gigantic celebration of mid-Victorian prosperity, confidence and invention at the specially built Crystal Palace

Fallen angel: Lucifer; the devil

Figaro: leading character in Rossini's opera

First Charles: English monarch whose reign led to the English Civil War, his own execution and the republic of Oliver Cromwell

Frock coat: a double-breasted coat with skirts extending almost to the knees, which are not cut away but of the same length in front as behind

Frouzy: dingy and damp

Genesis xl: 8, Genesis xli: 25: Joseph's interpretation of Pharaoh's dream

Goths and Vandals: destructive and ignorant barbarians

Grog: alcohol (perhaps rum and water in equal parts)

Hearsay evidence: what a witness has heard others say, but of which he has no personal knowledge

Heavy claims: pressing financial demands

Heerd un: heard him

Honduras: Central American republic

I am a Citizen of the World: *The Citizen of the World* by Oliver Goldsmith (1728–74)

In default of issue: there being no children from the marriage

Ingress: entry

In lieu of: in place of

Intercession: plea on behalf of somebody else

I would fain have: I would have wished/wanted to

John Bull: cartoon or caricature version of a typical Englishman

John Howard: (1727–90) Famous philanthropist and prison reformer

Kirkyard: churchyard

Life interest: not his to bequeath: his

property during his lifetime only

Litigation: the legal process

Loight: light

'Lubricating influences of oil gold': the power money can exert over the law. The law is imaged as a piece of unwieldy machinery

Measter: master

Mesmerism: hypnosis

Metaphysical conclusion: an over-subtle conclusion

Monomania: to be obsessed with one idea or subject

Morgue: place where dead bodies were displayed in Paris for identification

Mountebank: a quack (usually a market-place entertainer selling patent medicines or cures)

Nankeen: yellow cotton cloth, from the Chinese city of Nanking

Neapolitan: from Naples

Nigh on: very nearly

Odium: hatred

Open chaise: light carriage

Oratorio: semi-dramatic (i.e. not fully staged like opera) musical compositions based on scripture, with chorus, soloists and orchestra, e.g. Handel's *Messiah*

Order book: the driver's working list of clients' names, addresses, dates and times

Organ boy: organ-grinder, a familiar Victorian street entertainer, often a foreigner

Ottoman: a type of sofa, often with storage space inside

Out of livery: wearing plain clothes, not in servant's uniform

Particular: noticeable, with added sense of 'strange'

Pathetic apostrophes: moving cries or appeals

Pecuniary arrangements: money matters, i.e. Walter's salary

Père la Chaise: famous cemetery in Paris

Phlegm: coolness, dullness

Potentates: powerful Eastern rulers

Principal: the original sum of money

Privity: knowledge

Profaning marks: signs of pain and suffering

Quack: a pretender to medical skills

Radical: desiring change or reform (in the nineteenth century almost certainly a Liberal)

Raphael: famous Italian Renaissance painter (1483–1520)

Recitativo: a style of musical declamation, between singing and speech

Recording angel: angel in heaven who records all our deeds on earth

Recreant: faint-hearted

Rembrandt: great Dutch artist, particularly of portraits (1606–69)

'Rights of Women': Mary Wollstonecraft's 1792 publication – more than a century before women achieved the vote

Sanguine: hopeful, confident of success

Season: time of year when the fashionable world assembled in London

Seat: family home

Sexton: church official whose duties include ringing bells and digging graves

Sheridan: (1751–1816). Irish-born dramatist – *The Rivals, School for Scandal, The Critic* – who first coined the expression 'at a deadlock'

Solitary grandeur: it was customary in Victorian England for the ladies to leave the gentlemen on their own after dinner, while the latter enjoyed port or brandy and cigars

Solomon in all his glory: St Matthew vi: 28–9. The Sermon on the Mount

Sotto voce: in a quiet voice, almost a whisper

St Cecilia: patron saint of music

Straining: stretching the drawings over a frame

Subscription: money promised and paid

Summun: someone

Superscription: words written on the envelope

Surety: someone willing to pay bail for another

Surplice: loose white vestment, worn by clergy and choir

Talisman: a charm

Testimonial: letter of recommendation

T'ghaist: the ghost

The Smudge: a gentle dig (by Collins) at dealers' and collectors' gullibility

Tiglath Pileser: the name of several Assyrian kings

Titian: (*c*.1477–1576) great Italian Renaissance painter

Turnpike: a toll gate

Typhus: a contagious fever

Tyrol: province in Austria/North Italy; a popular resort for walkers, climbers and tourists

Vestry: small room attached to a church for keeping vestments, records and other valuables, sometimes used for meetings

Victor Hugo: (1802–85) French novelist, dramatist and poet

Wafers: used to receive the impression of a seal, like wax; or to attach papers or to seal letters

Waive: relinquish

Wanting: lacking or missing

Wreak it: to carry it out

Yander: yonder

Examination Questions

1. Either (a) Give an account of the events before the wedding of Sir Percival Glyde and Laura Fairlie which lead (i) Marian Halcombe and (ii) Mr Gilmore to feel deeply unhappy about the forthcoming marriage.

Or (b) What do you consider to be the outstanding characteristics of Count Fosco's personality? Substantiate your views by referring to incidents in which he is concerned.

(*Associated Examining Board, 1970*)

2. Either (a) Describe the character of Marian Halcombe. What is her importance in *The Woman in White*?

Or (b) What qualities make *The Woman in White* so gripping?

(*Associated Examining Board, 1981*)

3. Either (a) Basing your answer on specific incidents, explain whether you find Sir Percival Glyde or Count Fosco the more wicked.

Or (b) Do you think patience is Laura Fairlie's chief characteristic?

(*Associated Examining Board, 1982*)